You Can Earn Each Hour

$12 to $24

Or More

Playing Casino Craps

Zeke Feinberg

BEAT THE RECESSION CASINO CRAPS
EIGHTEEN WAYS TO WIN

TABLE OF CONTENTS

This book was
written in
SPITE OF MANY

The Author

BEAT the RECESSION . . .
BEAT the DEPRESSION

Earning Excellent Hourly Rates

WINNING at CASINO CRAPS

If you are trying to win over $100,000
per year — Don't buy this book

but

if $12 to $24 or more per hour is your lifestyle,
this book can help you.

CRAP BANKROLL

Good question! How much would a novice need for a CRAP bankroll to earn $12 to $24 per hour?

Answer: $600

Seems quite fishy at first. If you only "worked" ten hours, earning $120 to $240 per week, you would have a minimum return on your investment of 20 % plus comped extras per week! ! ! Excluding comps, this equates to over 1000 % per year. This is over ten times your original investment. The financial return percentage is much greater when you "work" more hours. It further increases when you abide by the guidelines suggested in this book. Leave greed to others who have their $600 CRAP bankroll completely exposed.

Feeling at ease at an excitable CRAP table can be most difficult and awkward for someone who has never uttered, "Six dollars each on the six and eight".

This is not our best wager, but for the inexperienced, it is probably the best wager for their first wager.

If the six or the eight is generated by toss of the DICE, instruct your dealer, "down on both the six and eight".

On the other hand, if neither place bets (6 or 8) are created by the DICE after three or four additional rolls, take a deep breath and tell your dealer, "down on both the six and eight".

Should your first wager be a loss, bide your time and relax. There will be many wagers, not all successful. But remember that charting, intuition flavored with a little superstition and the techniques learned will work to your advantage for the long term.

Now you should get into the tempo of the game.

Remember all of your wagers, including your original 'six dollars each on the six and eight,' are based on what the charting indicates, along with your intuition. Every wager will not always be a winning one. Every loss must be overcome with at least four wins.

It is my sincere statement, that in the long term, earnings of $12 and more per hour are attainable. Unfortunately not all will succeed. Those that fail will know it really wasn't the calls of the stickperson, but greed, lack of discipline or a combination of both.

Once you have depleted the entire $600 CRAP bankroll, *quit playing.* Casino CRAPS is not a game for you.

Do not add even $1 to your original Crap bankroll.

If you want to continue with the excitement, exhilaration, stimulation and mystification of the 'Arena of CRAP Action', then obtain this author's book "Casino CRAPS is not for gambling. Casino CRAPS is for exciting entertainment."

CASINO CRAPS IS A VICIOUS GAME

The casino's win percentage as represented by the New Jersey Casino Commission is approximately fifteen (15 %).

This fifteen (15 %) casino's win percentage is based on actual gross amount of cash and markers exchanged for gambling chips. The net amount of actual money exposed to the exciting, exhilarating game of craps is substantially less. (See article in this book about "Mistaken Identification"). This we will call the 'true drop'.

According to a fourteen month study by this author, the actual casino's win percentage of true drop exceeds 34 %.

WHY ?

The answer became obvious when I decided to study the *Game Of Casino Craps.*

Every author who has ever written about this fantastic exciting game recommends the identical methods to "win at Casino CRAPS".

They all repeat the identical garbage. If all these authors

agree on how to win at Casino CRAPS, then someone ought to explain why less than 1 % of Casino Craps players are overall winners.

The late John Scarne was the very best author and expert on all phases of gambling. His books, especially on DICE, inspired me to further investigate the game of CRAPS. Personally, I treasure his superb books on all types of gambling.

Okay, if you are satisfied to grind the casinos for $12 per hour to $24 per hour with a small gambling bankroll of $600 we can now proceed.

These methods can be applied to larger wagers to reap much more per hour, but that would be *gambling*.

I like to consider my techniques as *not gambling*, but more like *grinding the Casinos* for living expenses during this recession period. (If you are unemployed you are in the midst of a depression).

This author is the only CRAP author to state *"The only way to win at casino Craps is through the *green pastures of the Place bets"*.

As of this writing no one has developed a system or technique to win overall in the Arena of CRAP action. No one has put forth a workable money management system to win overall in Casino CRAPS.

*As in Green Dollar Signs.

That is why approximately five to eight out of a thousand CRAP players are overall winners. *This is less than 1 %.*

This means, that as of January 1992, there were 214 CRAP tables in the twelve Atlantic City Casinos. Most of these CRAP tables hold 12 *potential losers.* The fewer large CRAP tables allow 14 *almost non-existent winners* to participate in the exciting Palladium of CRAP Action.

Less than 2700 CRAP players are needed to have 100 % capacity at any one given moment. Of these 2700 potential victims of those dazzlin' DICE, only 81, or 3 %, would leave the casinos as winners. This equates to 97 % of the players lose their bankroll because they are uneducated in the Arena of CRAP Action. As these same 81 players play another day, or later sessions during the year, the overall winners will dwindle to about 24 from the original 2700. This is less than 1 % of our theoretical 2700.

The Hippodrome of Casino CRAPS is a dying gambling game. This is evidenced by the fact that before Donald Trump's Taj Mahal, the total number of CRAP tables in Atlantic City approached 250. The Taj Mahal added 30 more CRAP tables,

BUT

the total has dwindled to only 214. The Bally Grand and others are removing CRAP tables to make room for additional slot machines. Soon there will be less than 200 CRAP tables in Atlantic City. In the back of this book is a breakdown of the casino's win percentages for the various types of table games and the slot machines.

In Las Vegas most casinos have few CRAP tables. Steve Wynn's Mirage has 12 CRAP tables. Caesar's Palace has 13 CRAP tables. Many others have only one, two or three.

There are two reasons why this exhilarating game of CRAPS shows declining trends.

First Reason:

>A miniscule percentage of casino personnel and CRAP players really understand Casino CRAPS. This equates to less than 1 % of the Casino personnel able to give you a correct answer to specific question on the finer points of CRAPS.

Second Reason:

>Casino CRAPS is a very fast, confusing game. Old timers learned CRAPS in the streets and in the armed services. The younger generation

cannot cope with the variety of wagers and the speed of the game. No one can cope with the Casino CRAP'S appetite for devouring over 34 % of the players bankroll.

In a recent poll that I supervised, I asked 316 *Casino personnel two basic questions:

(a) What is the best wager in the Arena of CRAP Action ?
(b) Is it better to "buy" the place bets 4 or 10, or merely place bet the 4 or 10 if you intend pressing (increasing) these wagers when they become winners ?

Poll Results for (a) :

Pass Line Bet with Maximum Odds	87
Don't Pass Line Bet with Maximum Odds	229
Total Idiots	316

Poll Results for (b) :

"Buy" the 4 or 10	316
Place bet the 4 or 10	0
Total Imbeciles	316

Articles in this book will clearly explain that both the Pass Line and Don't Pass Line are **poor wagers**. The supposedly "true odds" is a trap for further transforming these **poor wagers** into **disastrous wagers**.

* Dealers, Floor Supervisors, Pit Managers, Shift Managers and top very highly paid Casino Executives.

Every other CRAP *author* (as in *authority*) stupidly claims the Pass Line and Don't Pass Line wagers are the very best in the Arena of CRAP action. They also state these wagers improve as you take or lay maximum odds. After reading the article in "Decreasing Percentages" you will understand why copy-cat authors are not the authority.

When making wagers on the Place bets 4 or 10 it is better to "buy" the first wager. To "buy" the 4 or 10 the player pays the casino a commission of 5% to obtain the true odds of 2 to 1, instead of 9 to 5. This is called vigorish in the Arena of CRAP action. The advantage on the first buy is less than 5% over Place betting the 4 or 10. After the very first win, the win factor increases dramatically in favor of Place betting the four or ten. As an example, compare the difference between "buying" the 4 or 10 and Place betting the 4 or 10. If a player is fortunate to overcome the odds of 728 to 1 for six fully pressed "buy" bets, compared to fully pressing the place bets, the advantage for the place bettor is 12.89 times greater than the "buy" bettor. Repeat: after beating the odds of 728 to 1 for winning six times on the 4 or 10, the financial return (per dollar invested) is thirteen times better for the Place bettor. This is thirteen hundred percent (1300 %) better. Every additional win further expands the Place bettor's advantage.

Not one person in the Arena of CRAP Action ever disclosed this fact. No one, not the authors, the experts or casino people even knew this fact.

Warning - this author *does not approve* of the 4 or 10 Place bets unless charting indicates a very rare wager is viable.

Repeat: CRAP Authors and Casino Personnel comprise the know-nothing-ism of the CRAPS society.

Following the advice that you read in previously written CRAP books will make you a loser.

Fortunately for you as a reader you will find this dazzling game of CRAPS very simple, and exciting fun-time. But BEST OF ALL, you will replenish your income. It's almost like becoming an employee of the Casino earning a 'Craps payroll', but without the deductions.

The downside of this Casino Craps payroll is that health insurance is not included. To offset this, increase your intelligent CRAP play timewise.

WHAT HAPPENS TO PLAYER'S CRAP BANKROLL ?

* Typical CRAP Session

Percentage of CRAP bankroll *lost*	Percentage of Players
100 %	27 %
50 %	35 %
20 %	16 %
10 %	11 %
0 % (Breakeven)	8 %
** Winners	3 %
	100 %

Percentages were obtained over a period of 24 months by periodically asking various players what the final financial results were the last session they played Casino CRAPS. By session it is meant the total time a CRAP player spent during a particular visit to the Atlantic City casinos. In some cases, it was a weekend, others varied from a few hours, four to six hours or in the case of novices, perhaps 15 to 40 minutes.

* Author's opinion. Please note that these percentages are not related to dollars loss.

** These are winners for a particular session.

Overall winners, during the course of time, *dwindle to less than one percent of all CRAP players.*

EARNING $ 12 TO $ 24 PER HOUR

In order to earn consistently $12 to $24 per hour, you have already accomplished Step # 1. *You purchased this book.*

Step # 2 Digest and fully *understand* certain segments of this book.

Step # 3 Glance-read quickly the entire book. No need to study or memorize anything, yet. Just be able to comprehend certain facts so that your intuitive impulses will have proper guidance. Then go back and read various parts of this book.

Step # 4 *Understand* why charting (including Super-Charting and Mega-Charting) is fundamental to earn $12 to $24 per hour. Fully comprehend until you believe that **charting is the first tool to success.**

Step # 5 *Actually chart* of the flow of DICE numbers *before* entering financial action.

Step # 6 Earning time - let the action begin in the exciting, exhilarating, dynamic, and explosive ARENA OF CRAP action.

Step # 7 If winning, *do not become greedy.*

Here is additional advice to assist you in winning, not losing, and earning $12 to $24 per hour:

Don't play when tired.

Don't touch alcoholic drinks.

Don't push your luck after goals are obtained.

Don't try to outsmart the DICE.

Be *consistent with wagering.* Increase dollar amount of wagers only after a win. In the beginning increase only Place bets 6 & 8. This would mean $12 each on the 6 & 8 and $5 each on 5 & 9, or $34 total.

Don't play after a heavy meal. You don't have to eat to the dollar limit of your comp. Request smaller dollar amounts of food comps, so you can eat lighter, but more frequently.

EIGHTEEN WAYS TO WIN

SIX WAYS TO LOSE

The only wagers I am concerned with are the Place bets. In the course of this book it is my hope to convince you that these are the only bets you should make. *Forget the rest of the table !* If you are wagering the 5, 6, 8 & 9 Place bets there are **eighteen ways for you to win** and only **six ways to lose**. But this is only the beginning!

To fully understand this analysis, imagine that when both DICE are thrown by the shooter, one of the pair of DICE (singular of DICE is called a DIE) lands first while the second DIE lands a split second later.

Therefore, if the first DIE lands with the number 1 up, the only way to lose would be if the second DIE landed with the number 6 on the topmost surface. Assuming you have Place bets on the 5, 6, 8, & 9, if the second DIE landed with the number 4 or 5 on the topmost surface you would win on either the 5 or 6 Place bets. Therefore, there would be *two ways to win and only one way to lose.*

Following this scenario, when the first DIE lands with the other numbers up, you can easily follow Table 1 (on page 32) that shows a total of *EIGHTEEN WAYS TO WIN AND SIX WAYS TO LOSE*, for these four Place bets.

I can hear the so called CRAP experts state that there is additional money at stake.

My retort, "Baloney "! Read on for an explanation. I have yet to meet or hear about *an expert on the game of CRAPS* who really *understands* the game of CRAPS.

Onward to earn $ 12 to $ 24 per hour.

Let's discuss the fact that there is more money at stake.

When playing the Pass line, lets assume $5 is the wager. To obtain a lower casino's win percentage, the players would have $10 at stake by taking double odds. Now the player is exposed to that nasty 7 for $15. The only way to win is to repeat the Point number. Depending upon the Point number there would be *three, four, or five ways to win* and *six ways to lose.* *Absolutely horrible. Actually, once the Pass line Point number is established, betting on the Pass line loses 59.39 % of the time.

The inside numbers (5, 6, 8, 9) exposes $22 of your CRAP bankroll — but there are eighteen ways to win and six ways to lose. Insurance factor of three to one, *and you can remove your wager anytime.* But not so for the Pass line wager.

There is another method of analyzing the validity of comparing the wagers on the inside numbers (5, 6, 8, 9) to that of the Pass line wager. Lets compare the percentages at the very instant the inside numbers Place bet is made, to the values of the Pass line once the Point number, (with no odds, single odds, and double odds) is established.

* According to the 1980 Probability Table there will be 1320 point numbers. Theoretically 784 point numbers will be losers and 536 will be winners.

$$\frac{784}{1320} = 59.39 \text{ %}.$$ Approximately 60 % of the 1320 Pass Line Numbers are doomed to be failures (Losers).

Two Ways To Win
only
One Way To Lose

Three Ways To Win
only
One Way To Lose

Four Ways To Win
only
One Way To Lose

Four Ways To Win
only
One Way To Lose

Three Ways To Win
only
One Way To Lose

Two Ways To Win
only
One Way To Lose

TABLE ONE

EIGHTEEN WAYS TO WIN, SIX WAYS TO LOSE

PLACE BETS: 5, 6, 8 & 9

1st Die	2nd Die Winners	Ways to Win	* 2nd Die Loser	Ways to Lose
1	4 - 5 * *	2	6	1
2	3 - 4 - 6 *	3	5	1
3	2 - 3 - 5 - 6	4	4	1
4	1 - 2 - 4 - 5	4	3	1
5	* 1 - 3 - 4	3	2	1
6	* * 2 - 3	2	1	1

Place Bet # = 5,6,8 & 9   18 Wins   Losses = 6

The remaining 12 possible numbers that can be thrown have NO EFFECT on the Place bets. They neither cause a win or a loss (2, 3, 11, 12, 4 & 10).

* There will be only one number on the second DIE to create a losing 7 total.

Place Bets:	4 - 5 - 6 - 8 - 9
	21 Ways to Win
	6 Ways to Lose

Place Bets:	5 - 6 - 8 - 9 - 10
	21 Ways to Win
	6 Ways to Lose

Place Bets:	4 - 5 - 6 - 8 - 9 - 10
	24 Ways to Win
	6 Ways to Lose

* Yes, better insurance ratios (Wins to Losses) but can be financially very treacherous ! ! !

DIAMETRICALLY OPPOSITE

The ideas in this book are *diametrically opposite* to what is generally considered to be the proper way to play CRAPS. If these so called experts had a sure-fire way of winning they would probably not share it with the public.

My curiosity in CRAPS is as a mathematical hobby and my interests are diversified. My primary income is derived from the manufacturing of transportation equipment. While writing this book, I have obtained copyrights on three games and have applied for two patents involving the parameters of the Game of CRAPS.

Talk is cheap. The final test will be if you as a reader of this book can change your status from that of a constant *overall loser* to that of an *overall winner ! ! !*

Let me attempt to put you on the right path of winning.

Before we continue, let's analyze the Place Bet combinations using the technique just developed. The results are as shown in Table 2.

CRAP TABLE LAYOUT

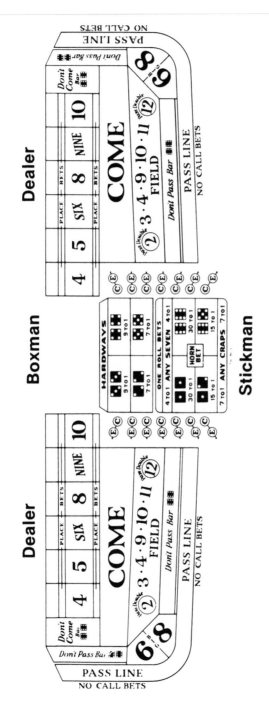

PLACE BET LAYOUT

CRAP TABLE LAYOUT AS VIEWED BY REBORN PLACE BET PLAYER

• No Pass Line • No Propositions • No Field, etc.

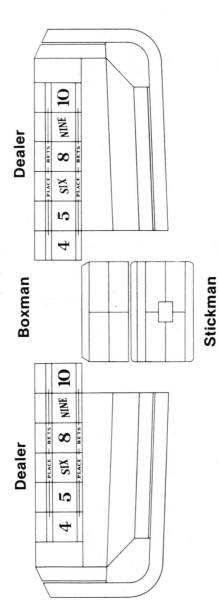

THE PLACE BET AREA

YOUR ONLY CONCERN

1. You **never** will be a shooter until you master the DICE Pre-sets -- At least six months away.

2. You **never** wager on the Pass Line or Don't Pass Line.

3. You **never** wager on the Don't Come or Come Bets.

4. You **never** wager on the proposition bets until six months down the road.

The only area of the CRAPS table layout that you play is the *Place bet area.*

The drawing of the CRAPS Table layout on the previous pages is self explanatory. One drawing shows the entire CRAPS table layout, the other shows *your play area.*

The variety of different wagers associated with the game of CRAPS are enough to frighten anyone. The only wagers we will participate in are those that are easy to understand and will make you a winner.

On the other hand, the inside (5, 6, 8, 9) Place bets are all you will need to understand to earn $12 to $24 per hour. And have fun too.

Therefore the game of CRAPS, as explained in this book, is all you have to know. It's enough to catapult you into earning $12 to $24 per hour.

The *unexplained* parts of the CRAPS table layout are best left unexplained.

BUT

this unexplained portion of the CRAP Table will teach you something very worthwhile. It contains possible wagers that only lead to financial ruination. Watch as others are tempted by these horrible wagers, only wind up as unhappy dismal losers.

As you start enjoying this new activity, earning a good lifestyle in the 'Arena of CRAP Action', you will need a driving force to make certain you don't go astray from your goal of $12 to $24 per hour.

There will be interesting periods when, after a win or two with charting and not wagering, to look around and observe how others are betting and losing. Also note the amount of various players rows of gambling chips.

Periodically players will replenish their diminishing row of gambling chips with fresh cash or markers. Watch their wagering techniques. Watch as they lose. And then, without any investment on your part, you will be self-taught to avoid the "unexplained area of the CRAP table layout".

MINIMUM PLACE BET WAGERS
and PAYOFFS

We will confine this discussion to the four inside Place bet numbers (5, 6, 8, 9). So far as we are concerned the 4 & 10 Place bet numbers are non-existent.

The minimum allowable wager on the 5 or 9 is $ 5. If these numbers are generated by our new friendly DICE then the pay-off is at the rate of 7 to 5, or $ 7 for any win. The true odds are 3 to 2, but in order to exist and make a profit, the casinos pay only $7 to maintain a win percentage of 4.00 % on either the 5 or 9.

For the Place bets of 6 or 8 the casino requires a minimum wager of $ 6 and the pay-off will be at the rate of $ 7 for each $6 bet. The true odds are 6 to 5, but since there is overhead, etc. with a $ 7 payoff for a $6 wager, the casino's win percentage is 1.515 %

Every other wager on the CRAP table layout holds no interest or direction on the road to earning $12 to $24 per hour. In fact the other possible wagers are worst than detours, they are formidable blockades.

There will be enough activity and excitement on every toss of the DICE to completely ignore these potentially expensive blockades.

Even when taking the Place bets down after a win, (or not having any place bet wagers), the excitement of our 'Arena of CRAP Action', is further enhanced as we chart our way to a knowledgeable, exhilarating conclusion. Winning !

While charting, and not wagering, don't be upset when, after removing your Place bets, a winning session continues as the shooter generates oodles of inside numbers.

So what - if you were available to wager continuously during the hot streaks, you would be flushed into the CRAPS *financial sewer* when the numbers generated return to "normal".

Watch the chips of others as they increase and decrease continuously, and then finally decrease at a slow pace until naught are left. The casino will *grind down and out* 97 % of these happy-go-unlucky CRAP players. The remaining 3 % of the winners today will dwindle to less than 1 % over the course of time.

Yes, less than one (1 %) percent.

Many of these CRAP players are entrepreneurs, doctors, lawyers and dentists. They are continuously losing, but they come back in droves, wearing a smile, coming and going; playing the same ole' stupid way ! ! !

THEORETICAL EXPECTATIONS

What is the Theoretical Expectation if a CRAP player placed the inside place bets (5, 6, 8, 9) for the minimum wagers and decided over the next four hours that these wagers would be in action 100 % of the time ? This meant that the inside place bets ($22) would be working all the time, even on the come out rolls. We will assume the numbers generated conformed to the 36 Probability Table.

Every 7 would cause a loss of the $22 which then would be replenished by the player. Any winning inside number (5, 6, 8, 9) would reward the player with $7 as the pay off is equal on all of the inside numbers at the minimum wager level.

$$\text{Time period} = 4 \text{ hours}$$
$$\text{Assumed Rate of numbers} = 144 \text{ per hour}$$

There are four series of 36 numbers per hour or a total of 16 series during the four hours of play.

From the 36 Frequency or Probability Table, there are 18 ways to make the four inside numbers:

	Ways to Win
Place Bet 5	4
Place Bet 9	4
Place Bet 6	5
Place Bet 8	5
	18 Total Ways to Win

There are 6 ways to generate a losing 7.

Net loss per series of 36 numbers
Losses: 6 x $ 22 = $ 132
Wins: 18 x $ 7 = $ 126

Net Loss per 36 numbers $ 6

Hence, over the four hour period where there are 16 sets of 36 theoretical numbers, the theoretical loss would be 16 x $ 6 or $ 96.

In order to have created a profit of $12 per hour, or $48 over the four hours, this player must find a way to make up the difference:

$$
\begin{array}{lll}
\text{Theoretical Loss} & = & \$\ \ 96 \\
\text{Desired Profit} & = & \underline{\$\ \ 48} \\
& & \$\ 144 \quad \text{Off Target}
\end{array}
$$

Obviously we cannot have our numbers active or working on every toss of the DICE, especially on the come-out-roll.

This obstacle has a very basic and simple solution. We must be very selective in our timing as to when to wager and when not to wager. Theoretically there are 18 inside place bets (5, 6, 8, 9) per 36 events, and 6 - 7's. In the one hour period there are four series of these events, totaling 72 inside numbers and 24 -7's.

Our goal would be to attain eight place bet wins against a maximum of two losses:

$$
\begin{array}{lll}
\text{8 Wins} \ @ \ \$\ \ 7 & = & \$\ 56 \\
\text{2 Losses} \ @ \ \$\ 22 & = & \underline{\$\ 44} \\
& & \$\ 12 \quad \text{earnings per hour.}
\end{array}
$$

We must find a method or technique to win 8 times, while losing only a maximum of 2 times. It appears that 8 wins out of 72 Place bet numbers per hour should be easy. But part of the 72 Place bet numbers are Pass line point numbers. Therefore, the selection of possible wins is reduced.

To offset the loss of Place bet numbers to the Pass line point number, we need as many tools possible to avoid the 7's. You can never eliminate the 7's, but sometimes, when you are a shooter, you might reduce the quantity of 7's. Postponing 7's for a long period of time is difficult and rare, even with good pre-setters.

As you read on, there are procedures and techniques to assist you in the 8 win to 2 loss goal.

Note: If 'not working' on the come out roll, normally the Place bettor has a slight advantage. One-sixth of the time a 7 will be called, but many shooters alter the frequency table to create more 7's than theoretically expected.

PLACE BET: 6 *OR* 8

Place Bet: EIGHT (8)

Ways to WIN:	(2-6)
	(3-5)
	(4-4)
	(5-3)
	(6-2)
	Five Ways
Ways to LOSE:	(1-6)
	(2-5)
	(3-4)
	(4-3)
	(5-2)
	(6-1)
	Six Ways

WAYS TO WIN
+ WAYS TO LOSE
———————————————
= NUMBER OF EVENTS.

The number of events that affect the outcome is the summation of the ways to WIN added to the ways to LOSE. Therefore, only eleven events will affect the outcome.

Win = 5   Lose = 6   5 + 6 = 11 events. The dollar value of the wager *does not* affect the value of the percentages.

Assume a $6 Place bet. Therefore the investment is $6 times the number of *events* that affect the outcome of the Place bet wager.

Investment:	$6 x 11 events	=	$ 66
* Return:	5 wins x ($6 + $7)	=	$ 65
Casino's Win		=	$ 1
Casino's Percentage		=	1.515 %

* Player's *return* equals the five ways to win $7 plus the return of your $6 Place bet. Therefore, player's return is 5 times $13 for a total of $65.

The same values are identical for the number six Place bet wager. Therefore the *casino's return* for the Place bets on six or eight *are identical.*

	Casino's Percentage
Place Bet 6	1.515 %
Place Bet 8	1.515 %

SIMULTANEOUS WAGERS

Many books on CRAPS state when two bets are made simultaneously, the casino's percentage remains the same as if each bet was individual.

This is outrageously incorrect.

This book on CRAPS will prove that as two bets are made, instead of one bet, the casino's percentage decreases dramatically ! ! !

When three or more bets are made at the same time, there is even a further decrease in the casino's percentage ! ! !

If more than 3 Place bets are wagered, you kill the casinos, but discipline is the key word. Don't be tempted by that Green Goddess of Greed. **Keep in mind your goal of earning $12 to $24 per hour.**

NO BOOK ON THE GAME OF CRAPS
EVER DISCUSSED OR ANALYZED THE
VALUES OF THE CASINO'S PERCENTAGE
WHEN VARIOUS COMBINATIONS OF
PLACE BETS ARE MADE.

OBVIOUSLY NO ONE EVER
INVESTIGATED THIS IMPORTANT
FACET OF THE GAME OF CRAPS.

In fact, previous authors stated that combining wagers had no affect on Casino's win percentages. This is why these previous authors **never understood CRAPS ! ! !**

COMBINING PLACE BETS: 6 *AND* 8

Let's analyze what happens to the casino's percentage when we combine the Place bets on 6 *and* 8.

Ways to win-Place bet eight (8)	=	5
Ways to win-Place bet six (6)	=	5
Total ways to win		10
Ways to lose (make a 7)		6
Number of events		16

Investment: 16 x ($6 + $6)   = $ 192
*Return: 10 x ($6 + $6 + $7)
            10 x ($19)   = $ 190

Casino's win   = $ 2

Casino's Percentage   =   1.0417 %
                        or 1.042 %

UNBELIEVABLE

* When a six or eight is made, the player receives a win of $7 plus the return of *both* place bets.

After a six or eight is made, *then remove both Place bets.* Also note that 'ways to win' (10) divided by 'ways to lose' (6) is greater than one, actually 1.67 to 1 *in favor of a win.* **This we call the insurance factor.**

This is tremendous ! ! !
We are now breaking the sound barrier.

Now we have
DRAMATICALLY and DRASTICALLY
LOWERED the CASINO'S ADVANTAGE
and
DOUBLED THE INSURANCE FACTOR

The important *difference* in the Casino's percentage is **not** the arithmetic *difference*:

Casino's percentage when placing an eight **OR** a six wager is 1.515%

Casino's percentage when combining the eight (8) **AND** the six (6) place bets = 1.042 %

	Casino's Percentage
Place Bet 6 **OR** 8	1.515 %
Place Bet 6 **AND** 8	- 1.042 %
Arithmetic DIFFERENCE	0.473 %

BUT ! ! !

Actually the Casino has an additional advantage of 45.4 % when the player places either the eight (8) **OR** the six (6) in comparison to combining **both** the eight (8) **AND** the six (6).

$$\frac{0.473 \%}{1.042 \%} = \begin{array}{l} 45.4 \% \text{ additional advantage for} \\ \text{the Casino} \end{array}$$

This is outrageous that no other book on CRAPS ever recognized this most important fact.

Now that we observed that combining these two Place Bet wagers (6 & 8) *reduces* the Casino's percentages drastically, let us also investigate the combination of any two other numbers, and its affect on the Casino percentages.

REMEMBER: After either the 6 **or** 8 is made, then **REMOVE BOTH** the 6 **and** 8 Place Bets.

We now have removed

45.4 %

from the Casino's advantage.

Combine the 6 **and** 8 bets until one or the other is made. Then **remove** both bets.

This reduces the Casino's advantage to

1.042%

I prefer the slow conservative more positive method. Make *one* profit per shooter. Remember, there are a-heck-of-a-lot more short rolls than the unusual long rolls ! I will later explain the principle of two or more profits per shooter.

* Good Technique to improve typical bad CRAP player - but not good enough to reach our goal of $12 to $24 Per Hour.

WARNING

GREATER DOLLAR EXPOSURE

Look at the Casino's Percentage Table. Please note as the player takes or lays more odds, the Casino's Percentage decreases. The player has to be exposed to a greater dollar wager in order to decrease the Casino's Percentage.

It is true here also.

If the player places a bet of $6 on the 6 *OR* 8, the Casino expects to win 1.515 % of the $6 bet or $0.0909.

* When both numbers are wagered until either is made, the Casino expects to make 1.0417 % of the $12 bet or $0.1250.

The dollar differential is **not** as important as **decreasing** the Casino's percentage, and **increasing** the chances of winning your bet from 5 out of 11 events to 10 out of 16 events.

Repeat:

Chances of winning a 6 *OR* 8 is 5 wins out of 11 events. By betting on **both** the 6 *AND* 8, the chances of winning have been dramatically increased to 10 wins out of 16 events.

* Insurance factor increases twofold. But the theoretical dollar loss is only an increase of 37.5 %. When we learn how to avoid the 7's, this will work in our favor.

PLACE BET 5 *OR* 9

Place Bet— Five (5) *or* Nine (9)

Ways to WIN   (1 - 4)
                           (2 - 3)
                           (3 - 2)
                           (4 - 1)

Four Ways

Ways to Lose - (by rolling a 7) can be made six ways

Ways to Win **plus** Ways to Lose = Number of Events

The number of events that affect the outcome is the summation of the ways to win added to the ways to lose.

Therefore, only ten events will affect the outcome.

Win = 4   Lose = 6   4 + 6 = 10 Events

Assume a $5 place bet. Therefore, the investment is $5 times the number of events that affect the outcome of the place bet wager.

Investment:	$ 5 x 10 events	= $ 50
* Return:	4 wins x ($5 + $7)	= $ 48
Casino's Win		= $ 2
Casino's Percentage		= 4.00 %

* Players pay-off equals the four ways to win $ 7 **plus** the return of player's place bet of $5. Therefore, player's pay-off is 4 ($12) or $48.

CASINO'S ADVANTAGE

Place Bet 5	4.00 %
Place Bet 9	4.00 %

Let's analyze what happens to the Casino's percentage when we **combine** the Place Bets on the five (5) *AND* the nine (9).

Away we go . . .

COMBINING PLACE BETS: 5 *AND* 9

Place Bets - Five (5) *and* Nine (9)

Ways to win Place bet 5	=	4
Ways to win Place bet 9	=	4
Total Ways to WIN		8

Ways to lose (make a 7)	6
Number of Events	14

Investment:	14 ($5 + $5)	= $ 140
Return:	8 wins x ($5 + $5 + $7)	
	8 wins x ($17)	= $ 136
Casino's Win		$ 4
Casino's Percentage		2.857 %

Again, Unbelievable ! ! !

To my knowledge not one book on the Game of CRAPS ever disclosed this fact.

We are about to change the way CRAPS is played. Instead of being a loser, you can enhance your chance of being a winner.

We are on the path to earning $12 to $24 per hour.

Let's continue with this very simple basic arithmetic:

Casino's Percentage

Place Bet 5 or 9	4.000 %
Combining Place Bets 5 and 9	- 2.857 %
Arithmetic Difference	1.143 %

The real difference is how it affects the Casino's percentage.

We are not as concerned with the arithmetic difference of 1.143 %

BUT

$$\frac{1.143\ \%}{2.857\ \%} = 40.0\ \%$$

This means the Casino has an additional advantage of 40.0 % when you place **either** the 5 *or* 9 in comparison to **combining both** the 5 *and* 9

After a 5 *or* 9 is made, **remove both bets.**
Note that as insurance factor increases 100 % the dollar exposure only increases 43 %.

PLACE BET: 4 *OR* 10

Place Bet - Four (4) *or* Ten (10)

Ways to Win   (1-3)
                  (2-2)
                  (3-1)
_____

Three Ways (3)

Ways to Lose (make 7)   = 6 ways

Investment:	9 Events x $5	= $ 45
Return:	3 wins x ($5 + $9)	= $ 42
Casino's Win		$ 3
Casino's Percentage		6.67 %

The same values are identical for the number ten (10) Place Bet wager. Therefore the Casino's win percentage for the Place Bets on 4 *or* 10 are identical.

Casino's Percentage

Place Bet 4	6.67 %
Place Bet 10	6.67 %

COMBINING PLACE BETS: 4 *AND* 10

Place Bets - Four (4) *and* Ten (10)

Ways to win Place bet 4	= 3
Ways to win Place bet 10	= 3
Total Ways to win	6
Ways to lose (make a 7)	6
Number of Events	12
Investment: 12 events ($5 + $5)	= $ 120
Return: 6 wins x ($5 + $5 + $9)	= $ 114
Casino's Win:	= $ 6
Casino's Percentage:	= 5.00 %

You are continuing on the road earning $12 to $24 per hour. This is only useful information. You must travel deeper into the valley of superior CRAP knowledge. Note that dollar risk increases only 52 % as insurance factor increases 100 %.

Dollar risk is casino's win percentage times players dollar exposure.

	Casino's Percentage
Place Bet 4 *OR* 10	6.67 %
Place Bet 4 *AND* 10	<u>5.00 %</u>
Arithmetic Difference	1.67 %

REAL DIFFERENCE

$$\frac{1.67 \%}{5.00} = 33.4 \% \text{ (actually 33.3 \%)}^*$$

This means by removing your place bets on the 4 *AND* 10 after one of these numbers is rolled you are NOT giving the casino a 33.3 % additional advantage.

---

[*] Arithmetically correct because we are "rounding up" decimals 33.4 % SHOULD BE 33.3 %. Just to make certain someone does not think we erred, as 1.67 % really is 1.66666.

BRIEF REVIEW

	Casino's Percentage
*Place Bet 6 *AND* 8	1.042 %
Place Bet 6	1.515 %
Place Bet 8	1.515 %
*Place Bet 5 *AND* 9	2.857 %
Place Bet 5	4.000 %
Place Bet 9	4.000 %
*Place Bet 4 *AND* 10	5.000 %
Place Bet 4	6.667 %
Place Bet 10	6.667 %

* Reminder: The arithmetic difference is important, but more important is the percentages we are taking away from the casinos.

This is a fuel and food stop on the road to Income Town, U.S.A.

COMBINING TWO PLACE BETS

I don't recommend these wagers, but let's quickly review them:

	Casino's Percentage
*4 AND 5	3.846 %
4 AND 9	3.846 %
10 AND 5	3.846 %
10 AND 9	3.846 %
4 AND 6	2.597 %
4 AND 8	2.597 %
10 AND 6	2.597 %
10 AND 8	2.597 %
5 AND 6	1.818 %
5 AND 8	1.818 %
9 AND 6	1.818 %
9 AND 8	1.818 %

If you want to earn an income, obviously the family of bets available with the 5, 6, 8 and 9 place bets are more desirable.

* The Place Bets we have combined so far are the "sister" bets. i.e. Only those bets with the same probabilities of occurring; 6 and 8, 5 and 9, and 4 and 10.

Now we proceed to

further reduce Casino's Percentage

and increase our insurance factor

Now that you understand that
combining two Place bets
drastically reduces the Casino's percentage,
lets continue even further
to lower their percentage

COMBINING THREE (3) PLACE BETS

Now we come to the meat of our techniques; the ability to work with those magical inside numbers - 5, 6, 8 and 9.

Let's analyze all possibilities:

Remember when one Place bet wins, **we remove all place bets.** Later we will have advance information to go for more than one win per shooter.

Combinations

5-6-8
5-6-9
5-8-9
9-6-8

There are only four variations possible from the four "inside" Place bets of 5, 6, 8 and 9 when placing only three place bets. These four variations actually breakdown into two different groups:

5-6-8 would be the same as 9-6-8

5-6-9 would be the same as 5-8-9

VERY UNUSUAL PHENOMENON

The casino theoretically expects to win the dollar wagered on any place bet times the applicable casino's win percentage:

Place Bet	Wager	Casino's Win %		Theoretical Casino $ Win
5	$ 5	4.0 %	=	$ 0.20
6	$ 6	1.515 %	=	$ 0.09
8	$ 6	1.515 %	=	$ 0.09

Casino expects to win per series of events = $ 0.38

By combining all three wagers (5, 6, 8) the casino theoretically expects to win $17 times 1.176 % or $0.20. This is less than the $0.38 it theoretically expects to win when the three place bets (5, 6, 8) are wagered individually. This is almost 50 % less, or the casino expects to win almost 100 % more, when not combined.

So let's proceed to find out the results.

PLACE BETS 5 AND 6 AND 8
& 9 AND 6 AND 8

Ways to Win Place Bet 5	= 4
Ways to Win Place Bet 6	= 5
Ways to Win Place Bet 8	= 5
	14
Ways to Lose (make 7)	6
Total Events	20

Investment:	20 Events ($5 + $6 + $6)	= $ 340
* Return:	14 Wins x ($7 + $17)	= $ 336
	Casino's win	$ 4
	Casino's Percentage	1.176 %

Doggone — Would you believe it ! ! !

* Return = $7 Win + Return of $5 + $6 + $6 = $17
on the 5, 6 and 8.

COMBINING THREE PLACE BETS

PLACE BETS 5 AND 6 AND 9
& 5 AND 8 AND 9

Ways to Win Place Bet 5	=	4
Ways to Win Place Bet 8	=	5
Ways to Win Place Bet 9	=	4
Total Ways to Win		13
Ways to Lose (make 7)		6
Total Events		19

Investment: 19 Events ($5 + $6 + $5)	=	$ 304
* Return: 13 Wins x ($7 + $16)	=	$ 299
Casino's win		$ 5
Casino's Percentage		1.645 %

Casinos, we gotcha good !

* Return = $7 Win plus Return of $5 + $6 + $5 = $16
on the 5, 6 and 9

BRIEF REVIEW

(Three Place Bets)

Place Bets	Casino's Percentage	* Insurance Factor
5 - 6 - 8	1.176 %	7 to 3
9 - 6 - 8	1.176 %	7 to 3
5 - 6 - 9	1.645 %	13 to 6
5 - 8 - 9	1.645 %	13 to 6

* Not where we want to be yet, but NOT a bad technique — three place bets.

I told you
so !

Let's go again
to see what happens
when the PLACE BETTOR
COMBINES FOUR PLACE BETS

HOME AT LAST ! ! !

COMBINING FOUR PLACE BETS
5, 6, 8 AND 9

Now we have strength:

Eighteen Ways to WIN
Six Ways to Lose

Insurance Factor $\dfrac{18}{6} = \dfrac{3}{1}$

Place Bets   5, 6, 8 AND 9

Let's not get greedy and try only for one win per shooter, until we obtain experience and additional knowledge.

This basic simple knowledge can assists us in obtaining financial goal of $12 to $24 per hour.

PLACE BETS 5, 6, 8 AND 9

Ways to Win   = 18
Ways to Lose = <u>6</u>

Total Events   24

Investment: = 24 Events ($ 22) = $ 528
* Return: = 18 Wins x ($ 29) = <u>$ 522</u>

Casino's win $ 6

Casino's Percentage   1.136 %

Win percentage for sacred pass line wager is 1.414 %

$$\frac{1.414\ \%}{1.136\ \%} = 1.2447$$

This reflects the casino win percentage for the pass line is 24.47 % higher than that of the inside numbers (5, 6, 8, 9). Plus insurance factor is tremendously more favorable.

* Return = $7 Win plus the return of $22 wagered = $29

* SUPERIOR PLACE BETS

PLACE BETS ON   5, 6, 8 AND 9

Casino's % = 1.1364   **Remove all bets after one win.**

Insurance 3.00 to 1

18 Ways to Win

6 Ways to Lose

```
┌─────────────────────────────────────┐
│              IMPORTANT               │
│    CRAPS IS FOR EXHILARATING         │
│   ENTERTAINMENT AND EARNED           │
│              INCOME                  │
└─────────────────────────────────────┘
```

* Highly recommended if affordable. Total minimum risk of
$22 necessary for goal of $12 to $24 per hour.

* COMBINING FIVE PLACE BETS

4, 5, 6, 8 AND 9 *or*
5, 6, 8, 9 AND 10

Ways to Win = 21
Ways to Lose = 6

Total Events   27

Investment: = 27 Events ($27) = $ 729
** Return: = 21 Wins ($34.29) = $ 720

Casino's Win $ 9

Casino's Percentage   1.235 %

Insurance Factor: $\dfrac{21 \text{ Ways to Win}}{6 \text{ Ways to Lose}} = \dfrac{3.5}{1}$

* Risky for earned income

** Return = $27 + $\dfrac{\$153}{21}$ = $27 + $7.29 = $34.29

($153 is the total pay-off for the 5 Place bets)

KILL THE
CASINO

COMBINE ALL SIX
PLACE BETS

Really should say "Grind the Casino". Only to be used for expanding income **when really far ahead of scheduled** $12 to $24 per hour. Could really hurt if loser, so be very, very careful. Remember there are certain devastating 7's with your name as target when you get cocky.

COMBINING ALL SIX PLACE BETS

Ways to Win	24
Ways to Lose	6

Events   30

Investment   30 Events x $ 32   = $ 960

Returns:

Number	Ways to Win		Payoff
4	3 x $ 9	=	$ 27
10	3 x 9	=	27
5	4 x 7	=	28
9	4 x 7	=	28
6	5 x 7	=	35
8	5 x 7	=	35
24		=	$ 180

* Plus   24 ($32)   = $ 768
                                      $ 948

Investment:	$ 960
Return:	$ 948

Casino's win $ 12

Casino's Percentage   1.25 %

* Refund to Bettor of $32 every time a Place Bet Wins

Not only is the Casino's Percentage
Fantastically Reduced

To **1.25** %

We Now Have
Tremendous Insurance
Against Losing

24 Ways to WIN

6 Ways to LOSE

These wagers should **never be attempted** without the three
schools of charting.

I ONLY recommend playing *all six numbers* at certain times.

If you are charting the flow of numbers, *or* if you observe that neither the 4 or 10 has appeared in a string of rolls (say 30 to 36 numbers) then **add** the 4 and 10 to the numbers you are playing.

Also, if one of the numbers (4 or 10) has appeared, but the other number has not, then add *only the one you think is due.*

I do this because I believe in the Equilibrium Principle. That in time, all the numbers will approach the Probability Table.

Optional Technique: If the point is included in the 5, 6, 8 & 9 omit the point number and add either a 4 *or* 10, or the 4 *and* 10, depending on flow of numbers.

* More for information, and possibly fun time. *Not recommended for income earners.* Several unexpected losses can result, and keep you from making $12 to $24 per hour. Maybe try it when strongly ahead.

What would happen to the Casino's Percentage if all the Place bets were of equal dollar value?

Let's find out.

The lowest equal dollar wager possible on each of the six Place bets is $ 30. Therefore for each event the total wager would be 6 x $ 30 or $ 180.

Investment: 30 Events x $ 180 = $ 5400
Returns:

Number	Ways to Win		Payoff
4	3 x $ 54	=	$ 162
10	3 x 54	=	162
5	4 x 42	=	168
9	4 x 42	=	168
6	5 x 35	=	175
8	5 x 35	=	175

$ 1010

* Plus 24 ($180)   = $ 4320 / $ 5330

Investment:	=	$ 5400
Return:	=	$ 5330
Casino's Win		$ 70
Casino's Percentage		1.296 %

* Return of original wagers when one of Place bet numbers is generated by DICE (6 x $30).

PLACE BETS ALL NUMBERS

Number:	4	5	6	8	9	10		
Ways to Win:	3	4	5	5	4	3	=	$ 24
Wager ($):	5	5	6	6	5	5	=	$ 32
Win per Place Bet ($)	9	7	7	7	7	9		
Total $ WIN:	27	28	35	35	28	27		$ 180

$$\text{Average WIN} = \frac{\$180}{24} = \$ 7.50$$

$$\text{Ratio} \quad \frac{\text{Investment}}{\text{Average Win}} = \frac{\$ 32}{\$7.50} = 4.267$$

This means if you bet *on all six Place bets* (4, 5, 6, 8, 9 & 10), and a 7 appears before you make a WIN on one of these numbers, you have **lost** the equivalent of 4.267 wins.

Your insurance of having one of the six Place bets win is excellent.

Ways to WIN	=	24
Ways to Lose	=	6
Total Events	=	30

OR 4 ways to win for every 1 way to lose

WARNING

MULTIPLE PLACE BETS are a SUPERIOR METHOD

BUT REMEMBER

The bad, ugly 7 will appear every *sixth* time towards infinity. It can appear anytime, especially when you don't expect it and when you can least afford it.

OMIT THE POINT NUMBER

There are two schools of thought in omitting the Point number.

My school of thought is that the pass line point *losses outweigh* the pass line point *wins* by more than 46 % (46.27 % to be more precise). We should use this knowledge to sometime omit the Point number if it is one of the inside numbers.

The second school of thought is *by omitting the Point number* we are *decreasing the insurance factor*, thus increasing risk of losing. This could be very intelligently overcome by using the chart method.

Sometimes we should wager on the 4 *or* 10, possibly the 4 *and* 10 Place bets, but this is extremely risky without chart knowledge. Charting is a unique subject in itself and my extensive book on CASINO CRAPS CHARTING is very revealing.

Hence, for all practical purposes that minimize risk factors, ALWAYS make Place bets on the four inside numbers, irrespective of Point number.

What to do for PLACE BETS

AFTER

Pass Line Winner makes new point.

This author is now adamant unless Pass Line winner has at least one 7 (natural) before a new or second Point is established - *no wagers are to be made.* I don't care if he makes many additional pass line winners. I am satisfied to sit shooter out.

Even if the shooter is on one of those *most unusual hot streaks,* I don't care ! ! !

I am content to be an observer and charter. This is so rare a situation that in the long run I am better off by biding my time.

Even if pass line winner has a natural 7 on the come out roll, I may sit out the balance of the roll when glancing at a chart.

FEELS GREAT
but
POOR RISK

When comfortably ahead and I want to play strictly for enjoyment, I will make all six Place bets. After each number is called, I would then remove that number.

Irrespective of the charts, I will attempt to win on all six Place bets. This attempt is *only* made after several consecutive wins, and when generously ahead.

Only once have I been successful in this attempt, but what an accomplishment.

Three times I had five wins. Twice I removed the sixth number, and I lost the sixth number once.

Many lucky times I had four wins. Sometimes I tried for more, but generally I removed all place bets.

Overall you would have to grade me on my lucky ability, not my smarts, as I am ahead in this endeavor.

This is **NOT** to be attempted for the $12 to $24 per hour journeymen ! ! !

WARNING - MULTIPLE BETS

Also, when you win more than one place bet, the player has greater exposure in event of a loss (the 7 unexpectedly and undeservedly shows up).

The method of wagering multiple Place bets is *still safer* than pressing Place bets.

Additional Place bets add insurance to our casino attack, and with charting our insurance factor further increases.

ENOUGH

ENOUGH

ENOUGH

Why is my technique better?

Very Simple.

My technique brings into the CRAPS game a most welcome word:

INSURANCE ! ! !

The risk is spread out over a variety of bets.

LESS RISK

MORE POSITIVE RESULTS

SURER PROFITS

PRESSING PLACE BETS

On an unusually long roll a player can increase his profitability dramatically by PRESSING the PLACE BETS.

I have witnessed successful long rolls, but disagree with this procedure. In the final analysis, the number of successful *press the Place bets*' actions are greatly *outweighed by the losses*. This is due to the shorter rolls when measured in terms of dollars won and lost.

For every long profit making roll, there are too many short rolls that more than offset the advantage of the long roll.

True, you can be fortunate to play and press when this unusual successful long roll is near the beginning of your play. But in order to stay a big winner you should quit when ahead a bundle.

There are many untold interesting stories about right bettors who pressed Place bets successfully, and those who failed.

At a recent snack at the counter of an Atlantic City Casino, I sat next to four men, three originally from Iran and an Oriental now living in Puerto Rico. They ran their $1200 pool of money, playing a very unusual press bet procedure, to slightly less than $150,000. This took place over four days at various casinos.

They only played the 4 and 10, starting with buying each for $25. Once one hit, they came down on both the 4 and 10. The next bet was a buy of $50 each on the 4 and 10. When one hit, they came down on both numbers. The next time the buy was for $100 each. They continued this procedure with tremendous success over the four day period. I never found out what was their largest wager.

I congratulated them and wished them good luck. Then I heard what I did not want to hear. The bundle of almost $150,000 had dwindled to slightly more than $10,000. Still a winner, but a foolish winner.

Alas, Woe is me Alhambra! This is seldom the case.

My final remarks about pressing Place bets is that there are some procedures more intelligent than others.

Many DICE experts are more qualified than this author, and if you must press Place bets, I suggest you read elsewhere for that information. I disapprove of this procedure.

Income seeking journeymen ($12 to $24 per hour) *never* press Place bets.

They say

"Right Bettors Die Broke."

This author says

"Press Bettors Commit Financial Suicide."

If, as a CRAP player, you want to make a real fast killing by pressing place bets, then God bless you.

The *one time* you make a "killing" will more than be greatly offset by the *many, many times* you will lose ! ! !

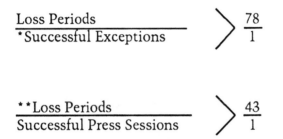

$$\frac{\text{Loss Periods}}{\text{*Successful Exceptions}} \quad \Big\rangle \quad \frac{78}{1}$$

$$\frac{\text{**Loss Periods}}{\text{Successful Press Sessions}} \quad \Big\rangle \quad \frac{43}{1}$$

*Money making rolls continuing after making Place bets in the middle of unknown rolls. (Middle of unknown roll is indeterminate).

** Money making rolls when pressing place bets at outset of very first place bet win *after* establishing pass line point.

These values are from personal charting records.

DON'T BE GREEDY

DON'T PRESS PLACE BETS

INCREASE VALUES OF PLACE BETS AT OUTSET

when predicted by

CHARTING

SUPER-CHARTING

and MEGA-CHARTING

THE CRAP PLAYERS *UNKNOWN CURSE*

If you heard it once, you heard it hundreds of times.

> **"Dice have no memory and
> every toss or roll of the dice is
> completely independent of any previous
> toss of the dice."**

This is the *curse* of all CRAP players.

* Because of this curse *all* crap players have *lost* quite a bundle of chips !

* Whenever CRAP players approach a table in the middle of an unknown roll and make sizeable wagers they will be **doomed.**

WHAT GOOD IS A COLD TABLE ?

It is a fact that every toss of the DICE is completely independent of any previous toss of the DICE and no previous toss or tosses of the DICE will affect the outcome of any future toss.

This is definitive. No Question ! ! !

BUT

If you were to go back ten or twenty years and hypothetically record every toss of the DICE since then, you would see a striking similarity for all the shooters rolls. This statement would be true if we were able to go into the future 5, 10, 20 or 50 years, and record all of the future shooter's rolls of the DICE at every casino.

The same would be the results of a hi-tech computer randomly selecting and recording millions and millions of numbers.

What are these similarities ?

By recording (charting) all of the shooter's rolls, we would quickly observe that the shooter does not hold the DICE very long.

Most shooter's rolls are very short, five or six numbers, ending in a pass line point decision.

There will be longer rolls, occasionally. Very rarely will there be one for one hour (approximately 130 to 140 total numbers).

When the DICE are very cold, you will notice that after the point number is established, a 7 is thrown almost immediately. Or, after a series of CRAP numbers, an 11 or the outside Place bet numbers (4 and 10) are tossed. In other words, almost always the cold table will certainly generate the devastating 7 before one inside number (5, 6, 8, 9) is called by the stickperson.

Instead, we are not really playing CRAPS according to Hoyle or Scarne. We are devoting talent, energy and money in an attempt to avoid the 7's.

Later in this book you will learn several additional techniques to avoid these 7's, but the tale of ice cold tables will teach us another way to avoid 7's.

Whenever a losing CRAP player bitches about his table being ice cold, he has a right to complain. *Ice cold tables* are when a point number is established and almost immediately a 7 is generated, wiping out the pass line wagers, the double odds wagers, and the place bets.

BUT

I have been present at *ice-ice cold* CRAP tables where the pass line points have only totaled possibly three or four wins to twenty and more pass line point losses. It's utterly disgusting to listen to the ugly and filthy curses of our financially harassed co-players.

How did I do while they were bitching? Not bad at all. One technique I use is never to wager until I chart at least 22 numbers. By doing this, I am not jumping into an unknown table. As I was writing this book, I reviewed six old charts at random that contained very ice cold results (for the right bettor).

When charting the flow of tossed numbers, I did not make any wagers until after at least 22 numbers were created. I would not make any wager until a point number was established followed *quickly (within 2 to 3 additional tosses)* by an inside number (5, 6, 8, 9). Then I would only wager the minimum $6 each on the 6 and 8. I would do this even if the point number was either the 6 or 8 and the inside number generated within two or three additional tosses was the other number (6 or 8).

This singular technique has earned money for me as rows of gambling chips from our co-players were devoured by the dealers.

At first, after possibly three or four additional tosses, and no 6 or 8 showed up, I will remove my wagers on the 6 and 8. If these numbers are later hit (won) before the 7, it doesn't matter. At least *maybe* the table is turning luke-warm.

This one, very simple technique, has not only saved me oodles of chips, but has created profits during the most adverse conditions.

Remember, we do not want to play CRAPS in the 'Arena of CRAP Action', as it is presently played by the present losers (99 % of all CRAP players)

We want to find techniques and methods to

A V O I D   T H E   S E V E N S .

Over ninety percent of all CRAP players *remain at risk* until the end of the shooters roll.

While all this exciting action is going on you should be a spectator. A very patient spectator. Because, if you can maintain a ratio of wins to losses exceeding 4 to 1, you will be earning income.

Imagine, an income with no bosses. Possibly two free (non-fattening) comped meals. Wagering $22 on the inside numbers is sufficient for most rating guidelines.

Let's now review what occurred on the six ice cold charting results that were obtained randomly from a large drawer full of my charts.

I won on all six occasions. My very first wager took place as follows:

	Number of 1st Wager	
Old Chart # 1	38 th	
Old Chart # 2	24 th	
Old Chart # 3	31 st	
Old Chart # 4	68 th	oh-so-cold
Old Chart # 5	47 th	
Old Chart # 6	41 st	

Smart yes, but lucky also, I won five times on my very first wager, lost once. In fact I went for two wins nine times and only lost $6 each on the 6 and 8. This gave me $63 - $12 or $53 **ADDITIONAL PROFIT.** All won because my mega-charting combined with my super-charting indicated two things:

(1) Future rolls should be heavy for the inside numbers.

(2) 7's were running at the rate of about one in four, so the future theoretically would be poor in 7's.

The most important factor, in addition to charting, was my patience in waiting for the right time to test the water temperature. Pardon me, I meant the *temperature of the table.* It was becoming luke-warm.

As an observer at a $25 minimum wager table I decided to chart because there were a few interesting high-rolling characters. This took place at the Taj Mahal in early February 1992.

Two of the high-rollers (characters) were wrong bettors. This table was oh-so-cold, I could not believe it. The first 64 numbers produced 28 - 7's. Unbelievable, but true. If this were a $5 minimum table, I would not have made *any* wager until the 83rd number.

Six players, never playing any proposition bets, tossed the DICE at a very high rate, 197 numbers in one-hour and one minute.

You would think the wrong bettors had a hey-day. They didn't. One was playing with $500 and $100 chips laying no odds. The other had an average $50 Don't Pass and layed single odds. I have never charted anything like this before, or witnessed as a spectator this type of result.

Here is the chart through the first eleven pass line point decisions:

		*	**
L-1	7-7-9-10-7	3	5
L-2	7-8-3-7	5	9
L-3	12-6-5-7	6	13
L-4	7-4-5-8-2-7	8	19
L-5	7-10-3-3-12-7	10	25
L-6	7-12-9-4-4-10-7	12	32
L-7	7-3-9-10-4-10-7	14	39
L-8	7-7-6-3-2-12-4-7	17	47
L-9	7-7-12-7-7-7-8-7	23	55
L-10	7-7-12-8-7	26	60
L-11	7-9-3-7	28	64

Pass Line Point Wins	0
Pass Line Point Losses	11
Come Out Roll Winners	17 (Losers for wrong bettor)
Come Out Roll Losers	5 (Winners for wrong bettor)
Stand-offs (12)	4 for wrong bettor
Elevens	0 (unusual, but it happens)

This was one of the three times during the past two years at Atlantic City casinos where I was suspicious of *defective DICE*. The other two times the quantity of 7's came very close to being one-sixth of all the numbers within a reasonable time.

* Running total of quantity of 7's.
** Total quantity of numbers generated by the DICE.

At the 197th tossed number the 7's totaled 44, but after 262 tossed numbers, the 7's totaled 48. These totals took place over one break (no $25 players) for about twenty minutes. At the 262 level the 48 - 7's are only 4 off theoretical. I was satisfied and left for a $5 table.

If I had stayed and played at this table (if it were a $5 table), and started playing slowly at the 83rd number, it would have been modestly profitable.

Here is the frequency of the first erratic 64 numbers:

Number	Frequency
2	2
3	6
4	5
5	2
6	2
7	28
8	4
9	4
10	5
11	0
12	6
	64

(What a time not to be a typical CRAP player !)

For very cold tables, the charting techniques will really assist in earned income.

WAIT

**Another Friend Is Going
To Enhance Our
Chances Of Earning
$12 to $24 Per Hour**

Our Most Important Chart

CHARTING

This is the most important singular chapter of this book ! ! !

EVASION, YES AVOIDANCE

In order to be in a posture to earn $ 12 to $ 24 per hour you will need all the tools available. Our attack on Casino CRAPS is actually an evasion *not an invasion*. Sounds contradictory !

A better choice of etymology would be *avoidance.*

Yes, avoidance.

From an ancient language meaning: ***avoid - dance.***
Avoid the 7's - Don't Dance around the table. Stick to your game plan and charting.

This book will *not* assist you in playing CRAPS as it is **improperly played** in today's 'Arena of CRAP Action'. That's why there are over 99 % losers ! ! !

Forget any information you may have read or heard about the Game of CRAPS.

Our approach will be to find various methods, techniques and superstitions to avoid the 7's. This will minimize the appearance of those financially destructive 7's.

You will never eradicate the 7's. All you want to accomplish is simply to obtain **four Place bet wins for ever singular losing 7.** Therefore our goal will be to avoid some of those critical 7's.

Besides being the most important chapter of this book, *CHARTING* is also the most prolific. Prior to re-writing the introduction to charting, 79 type-written pages on this subject were compiled plus an additional 40 odd handwritten pages. The end result was that several salable games on CRAPS were created and two patent-pending CRAPS "inventions" developed.

There are many ideas yet to be explored in the field of charting. So many in fact, there will be more than enough for a fair-sized volume.

Therefore, only the important basics will be thrust in your direction at this time. You will be amazed at the ideas you will create to intuitively interpret your charts.

Let's begin

Charting is compiling the flow of DICE numbers generated as the various shooters toss the DICE against the furthest padded wall.

Recall the CRAP Player's CURSE:

"Dice have no memory and every toss or roll of the dice is completely independent of any previous toss of the dice."

If the CRAP players curse is correct, can the compiling the flow of past numbers assist us in projecting future outcomes ?

YES !

YES ! !

OH MY, YES ! ! !

CAN CHARTING REALLY HELP ?

How can previous charting be of any assistance ? This is a very fair and valid question.

If we were able to chart the CRAP action generated numbers for all the CARP tables in the world for the next five or ten years, or go back in time and recapture the charting of all Las Vegas CRAP action for one day or 10 years, we would be amazed at the similarity of the charts.

These charts would include many of those once-in-a-lifetime so called *hot streaks.*

They would also include too many of those heart-breaking cold streaks (for the right bettors).

What does the charting REVEAL ?

By compiling the series of numbers generated by those intriguing DICE, certain predictions can be made. This will *minimize our loss periods* and **maximize our profit periods.**

This procedure is called CHARTING. Charting is accomplished by observing live CRAP action at the casinos. It also can be obtained by randomizing CRAP numbers on computers, or compiling numbers in the CRAP game called Pass Line Craps.

CHART READING

Chart reading is meant to be only *'glance read'*. **There is no need to study your chart.**

Just by 'glancing' at the chart you will gather sufficient information to act accordingly. A glance reader is as effective, as if the rolls generated were to be used as input to a high-tech computer. In this case, however, the computer is your brain.

NO COMPUTER CAN ACCURATELY PREDICT WHAT THE NEXT NUMBER OR NUMBERS GENERATED WILL BE TOSSED BY THE SHOOTER.

Your glance reading will give you a *good intuitive feeling* for the future outcome.

There will be *failures*, but the *successes* will greatly outnumber the failures, by at least a 4 to 1 ratio.

Once it's realized that shorter rolls greatly exceed the longer rolls (by at least 43 to 1), then you are on the way to profitable playing, earning $12 to $24 per hour.

**PROFITS
WITH
PLEASURE**

I know I don't have to tell you that *generating profits is much more desirable than creating losses.*

BUT! ! !

Generating profits while having fun amidst an exhilarating, mysterious atmosphere is the greatest. Especially when 'more experienced' CRAP players are losing their little bundles to the casino's percentages.

All this while you are earning $12 to $24 per hour ! ! !

Previously stated, almost of a ream of paper has already been used for the amplification of charting. You, as a provider of the good things of life (earning $12 to $24 per hour), will only need a few simple facts to get on with the excitement in the Hippodrome of CRAPS.

It will be best to chart, Super-chart and Mega-chart, and you must chart to earn consistent income

Charting is to compile the continuous flow of numbers generated by everyone.

Super-charting is maintaining a running total of Sevens (7's) as compared to **all the numbers.**

Mega-charting is keeping a running total *of the inside* **numbers (5, 6, 8, 9)** and comparing this with the running total of all numbers.

Our 36 Probability Table indicates that there will appear six number 7's out of every 36 numbers thrown. This equates to one-sixth of all numbers, in time, should be a 7.

The inside numbers (5, 6, 8, 9) have a frequency of appearing eighteen out of the thirty-six numbers thrown. Therefore, norm is one-half of the total numbers.

The principle attached to all phases of charting is that "in time" everything should be what is expected, as per the 36 Probability Table.

During fifteen years of charting, it is clear that within a reasonable time (up to two hours) these numbers have a pattern. They are askew, either above or below what the probability table predicts. Then they are in "tune" as per the probability table. Once they are on "target" as predicted, the inevitable occurs - they are askew again, or out of balance. This is an ongoing situation: On target - out of balance - on target - out of balance, etc.

Ninety-five (95 %) percent of the time this will occur within a reasonable time. The other five (5 %) percent of the time the erratic numbers go off in a tangent. The onslaught of too many 7's make the chart appear erotic or even erosive.

By coping intelligently with the 95 % element of time, earnings can be consistently maintained,

BUT

even during the other 5 % time element, earnings can be maintained, but at a much slower pace ! ! !

Even at a very, very ice cold table *earnings can be maintained if your charting is properly interpreted.* It can be done. It is being done. No one else at the table is smiling (right bettors), because no one else at the table is charting.

We must take a disadvantage in life and turn it into an advantage. Charting will do this — exchange an erratic flow of numbers into profits.

One book that really is amazing and impressive is "Innumeracy" by John Allen Paulos. His writings makes you put your thinking cap on.

The same approach should be taken here.

Look at your various charts, before you delve into the financially crunching world of CRAPS.

Analyze your charts when playing. If you are going to succeed you must have

PATIENCE,
DISCIPLINE,
LACK OF GREED

and a bit of intelligence- not mathematically or scientifically - just plain ole' common sense and street sense.

The ocean of CRAPS is yours to swim, wade or drown ! ! !
Think - but use your head.

Above all don't be greedy. Be disciplined ! ! !

If you have any additional questions, write to us at:

Hi-Lo-Yo Publishing Company,
P.O. Box 711,
Skippack, PA 191474-711.

Please include a self addressed envelope.

Lets continue onward to assist you in earning $12 to $24 per hours.

You, as a potential provider of income, must add that all important blending ingredient in addition to

Patience, Discipline, Lack of Greed

PLUS

INTUITION

SUPER-CHARTING 7's

Super-Charting is compiling on an ongoing basis the number of 7's generated by those excitable DICE, in comparison to the total numbers generated.

We will concern ourselves only with three conditions:

(1) Ratio of sevens (7's) to total numbers generated is approximately one-sixth. This is the theoretical ratio. Just a normal relationship.
(2) Ratio of sevens (7's) to total numbers that *exceed* the theoretical one-sixth ratio.
(3) Ratio of sevens (7's) to total numbers that are *less* than the theoretical one-sixth ratio.

We must remember that on any given toss of the DICE the odds of a seven being thrown is 5 to 1, or basically one in every sixth toss by the shooter.

There will be times when the toss of the DICE will result in a disheartening 7, but we must remember that by **super-charting,** our gains will outweigh the losses by at least a four-to-one ratio.

Let us consider the condition when the 7's generated the approximate one-sixth ratio. This is theoretically expected. When the ratio approximates the one-sixth status, I find the road to financial success easier. Many times I go for two wins. The critical decision is then placed on the *mega-charting.* This is the relationship of the inside numbers (5, 6, 8, 9) to the total numbers.

When the 7's exceed the one-sixth ratio by a considerable factor, such as 25% more than theoretical, then I loosen my purse strings. There should be more inside numbers coming out. Wagers will be made for the future should be rich in inside number. This would be an ideal time for two wins with the same shooter. Especially if the inside numbers are less than one-half of the total numbers. *This condition should expand your earning income time. Don't get greedy.*

Opportunities like this sometimes permit second and third wins at lower dollar risk values.

On the other hand, when the ratio of 7's is low in comparison to the theoretical one-sixth then **BEWARE**. Once the worm turns, the 7's will tend to balance out, and the amount of inside numbers will diminish. The chances for one win will decrease. *Watch the charts.* Hot streaks are surely rare, but when they occur they will be followed by cold streaks. It appears to me that after cold streaks, hot steaks *do not always begin.* But a period of stabilization may set in with possibly a slightly higher rate of 7's appearing to create a period of equilibrium.

Let's review one critical point when the 7's greatly outweigh the theoretical ratio of one-sixth. Obviously the more 7's, once the point number is established, the colder the table. Yes, earnings can continue BUT you must make certain that one inside number appears after the point number is established. Wager cautiously, possibly only on the 6 and 8 (even if point number is 6 or 8), until your winning ways continue in spite of the abundance of 7's. Remember, one of the inside numbers (5, 6, 8, 9) *MUST* appear once within three or four rolls. Rely on intuition based on chart reading.

Glance read the charts.

Lead not your wagers into temptation.

Don't be Greedy, have patience.

MEGA-CHARTING

Mega-Charting takes a few seconds per shooter's roll. It is simply maintaining a running total of the inside (5, 6, 8, 9) numbers. There are eighteen ways to make these inside numbers, or *ONE-HALF* of the 36 numbers possible.

Glance reading the ongoing running total and comparing this total to the total numbers generated gives you an excellent feeling on how and when to wager, or increase or decrease wagers.

This author believes in the EQUILIBRIUM PRINCIPLE. The numbers generated are very erratic, but they continuously become more consistent with the frequencies expected. And they also consistently get out of balance. The inside numbers (5,6,8,9) can be made 18 ways. Since this is one-half of the 36 combinations possible, norm for the running total for the inside numbers would be one-half of the total numbers. During the course of CRAP action the running total for the inside numbers may approximate one-half of the total numbers generated, but in the main these inside number totals will be higher or lower than the one-half expected.

When the running total for the four inside numbers (5, 6, 8, 9) exceeds 50 % of the total numbers by *more* than theoretical, then it is unlikely that future tosses will be rich for profitable inside wagers. Conversely, when the running total of the inside numbers are much *less* than what theoretically should be expected, then it should be income earning time.

But all of this is nonsense unless two factors are primarily considered. Put no weight in this analysis unless there are at least 40 numbers under your belt. The greater the number of total numbers, the greater the tendency for accurate assumptions.

Now comes the killer!

All of the previous is *only useful if the quantity of 7's are one-sixth or more than what you expected.* Repeat ! ! ! This is the critical decision maker. Expected future rolls should be poor in 7's.

This is a glance-reading technique, not an arithmetic session. Mega-Charting is another tool towards earning $12 to $24 per hour.

Remember — only a few seconds is required after the shooter's roll ends (in a decision) to mega-chart.

THE CRITICAL DECISION MAKER FOR MEGA CHARTING IS THE VALUES OF 7's.

THE HIGHER THE RATIO OF 7's ABOVE ONE-SIXTH AVERAGE, THE BETTER THE OPPORTUNITY FOR EARNING AN INCOME.

If you were to plot a graph showing the relationship of both the quantity of 7's and the inside numbers, to the total numbers called by the stickperson, it would be clear that these ratios are never exactly as theoretically expected over an extended period of time.

What is theoretically expected ? The quantity of 7's should be one-sixth of the total DICE totals while the inside numbers

(5, 6, 8, 9) should be one-half of the numbers generated.

This author strongly believes in the Equilibrium Principle which clearly states that 'towards infinity, all of the numbers generated by all the DICE will conform to the frequency expected' as per the probability table. In the short time frame, there is a tendency that 95 % of these numbers remain reasonably close to what is expected. But continuous deviations will occur. There will be a surplus, or a deficit, in the quantities expected on an almost continuous pattern.

Because it is expected that these trends will have continuous approaches or crossing of the equilibrium points of the graph, you, as a bettor, will have to obtain information by charting. This will give you information as to when to avoid wagering, when to minimize wagering, when to attempt the second win and even when to increase your wagers (after a win, naturally).

CHARTING PAD FORMAT

Casino	*Taj Mahal*						Date	5-20		Start	2:10		End						
L	W	1	2	3	4	5	6	7	8	9	10	11	12	13	14	15	16	17	Inside #	7's	Total #
L		⑧	3	2	6	9	7												3	1	6
L		7	⑨	5	10	10	8ₕ	7₀₅											6	3	13
L		④	11	7															—	4	16
	W	12	⑥	8	6														9	—	20
L		⑤	3	9	3	7ₙₛ													11	5	25
L		⑩	8	5	7														13	6	29
	W	11	⑤	4	5														15	—	33
	W	⑨	5	9															18	—	36

Designations:

⑨ Circled number is point number

H Hardways 4, 6, 8 & 10

NS New Stickperson

DD Dropped DIE or DICE

OT Off Table

CS Corner Shooter

PS Pre-Set Shooter

EQUIPMENT NEEDED TO CHART NUMBERS

All you need is a pen or pencil and a 3″ x 5″ or 4″ x 6″ spiral pad.

I prefer a ball point pen. Pencils may lose their points. These spiral pads generally have 50 to 60 sheets at a minimum.

One spiral pad will very easily last a minimum of 25 hours of exciting CRAP action.

A pre-printed 4″ x 6″ charting pad that has provisions for charting, super-charting and mega-charting is available. This easy to use pad also contains Zeke's techniques and charting samples.

Contact:
Hi-Lo-Yo Publishing Company
P.O. Box 711
Skippack, PA 19474-711.

TIME TO CHANGE CRAP TABLE !

There is a continuous movement of CRAP players going from one table to another, then yet another praying and hoping to find that rare long "hot roll" or at least a "warmer table".

I call this the "Moment of CRAP Inertia". A player who is losing in the Arena of CRAP Action, will continue to lose, irrespective of how many CRAP tables are visited.

This is a simple obvious statement since less than one percent of the CRAP playing population can claim they are a possessor of the victory flag. Winners, when they exist, know what they are doing and don't depend upon table changes. They depend upon their own talent, self-discipline and the absence of greed.

A famous story, "Acres of Diamonds" illustrates that green pastures abound and it is foolish to look elsewhere, such as your neighbors green pastures.

BUT

there is a time to change CRAP tables, very effectively.

Even when winning, I have repositioned myself to other tables for future strategy. A typical example only occurred a week before this book went to the printer. While charting and playing this income rich particular table, the profits were consistently fruitful. In fact the first seventy-four numbers produced only four 7's, one arriving during a come out roll. This was a tepid table for five other right bettors, while two small wagering wrong bettors suffered the wrath of the place bet numbers.

Relying on the principle of equilibrium I put myself on "7 Alert". Even though winning at higher levels intuitively called, "$22 on the inside numbers". The last three wagers were at much higher levels of $22 multiples. A series of CRAPS and 7's developed. "Down on the 5 and 9." I should have also removed the 6 and 8. "7." Now I was on 7, red alert. After two CRAP numbers and one come out roll 7, the point number was 6. One more CRAP number then the expected 7. Fortunately I made no wagers. I quit wagering, but continued to chart. There were now seven of those evil 7's (actually six, since one was a come out roll) out of a total 82 numbers. Because I discontinued wagering, I made a time notation. The next twenty-two minutes developed 51 additional numbers concluding in very, very short rolls ending in fifteen additional 7's.

This was an unusual break down of the fifty-one numbers.

Point Numbers	=	15
Come Out Roll Sevens	=	1
Losing Sevens	=	15
Elevens	=	4 none on come out roll
CRAP Numbers	=	11
4 and 10	=	5
5, 6, 8, 9	=	None after point numbers
Total Numbers		51

Even if an inside number had appeared, my wagering time for this table, at this time, was finished.

This is when you relocate to a new table, on a "winning inertia" combined with "7 ALERT".

This would be an ideal time to repeat the "DICE PLAYER'S CURSE":
> **"Dice have no memory Every toss or roll of the Dice is completely independent of any previous toss of the Dice."**

Charting can never be an exact science, but Charting can be a winning science.

CRAP LOSERS

This author believes that there are only five to eight winners out of one-thousand CRAP players is a fairly accurate statement.

Therefore when you walk into any casino's 'Arena of CRAP Action', all those involved are effectively *overall losers*.

If a casino has ten CRAP tables operating at full capacity of twelve losers per table at any given time, then 120 CRAP players are present.

It would take approximately eighty CRAP tables, fully engaged, to hold about one-thousand players.

YET, Imagine

ONLY FIVE TO EIGHT OVERALL CRAP WINNERS WOULD BE PRESENT !

It won't be any of those *HIGH-ROLLERS !*

It won't be any of those smug *WRONG BETTORS !*

It won't be that *screaming CRAP player* who just won $18,000 during several most unusual lucky streaks.

It could be a Doc Grafstein (Doctor of CRAPS). It could be a sly, quiet, older man, minding his own business, but carefully watching the DICE. A man who is choosing his wagers very wisely, playing possibly with the cycles, and **quitting** when his goal is attained. Above all, his wagers will be small or medium sized (green chip or two) periodically.

It won't be the *pass line bettors.*

It couldn't be the *pass line bettors taking full odds.*

It positively will never be one of those characters who are *forever pressing their fate by pressing their place bets.*

It will virtually never be a *vigorish player* of the 4 and 10 who presses them. Unaware that after the very first "buy" bet, the financial return is far superior if the 4 and 10 were placed rather than "bought". It doesn't really matter, though, this type player is doomed for the *financial sewer,* either way they play.

It is that bag lady Lucy I observed at the Taj Mahal. She only played at tables with very few players so she could shoot very frequently. Lucy only made a red chip ($5) bet when she was the shooter. Now here was the very best pre-setter I have ever seen. Full story is in later book. She was certainly better than me.

In the Bible of CRAPS, it very clearly states, "He who plays the pass line with full odds, and at every opportunity, or at least twice, makes a come bet with those foolish maximum odds, shall reap the wrath of the 7's, when all the come bets *COME TUMBLING DOWN*". This player would never even qualify in theory to be an overall winner.

It certainly is not one of those CRAP authors who are spilling their guts telling you, how to win or beat the casino.

It will never be a casino CRAP dealer, stickperson, box person, floor supervisor, pit boss or a chief executive in full command of his own gambling scene, when they travel out of town to gamble.

It will never be a mathematics professor of a major university who ran 5,000,000 CRAP computations on a high-tech university computer. This character raised $20,000 among his friends, associates and other gamblers. Then went to the Showboat in Atlantic City and with all his mathematical knowledge made the $20,000 look like six white chips - $6.

Writing about math professors - during the past few years, I became friendly with three other math professors. They were addicts of the game, and all three happened to be winners during the CRAP sessions where we met. All three were ahead, playing the pass line with full odds. When I inquired about their overall lifetime status as being a winner or being behind (some don't like the word LOSER) here were the responses:

(1) "Even though I'm not a complete winner, the only way to play is the pass line with full odds."

(2) "I'm not there yet, but give me time. The very lowest mathematical win percentage one can get."

(3) "Ahead today and my last trip — best way to play." (pass line with full odds).

What does all this mean ? It means that you will be playing smarter and becoming a convincing winner, while inhaling the call of the wild (stickman's call) — and earning el dinero.

WHY NOT INCREASE HOURLY RATE OF PAY ?

Once you are on stream earning your desired rate of CRAP play, $12 to $24 per hour, and your greedy monetary appetite urges you to go to a higher rate of CRAP earnings, then the inevitable will occur.

You will be doomed to be a loser.

In order to increase your level of CRAP earnings, one of two procedures, or a combination of both, must change.

The level of wagers must be increased or more wagers must be exposed to those devastating 7's each hour. *Either, or both will positively kill your chances of earning your goal of $12 to $24 per hour.*

Ask yourself "if these techniques work for one level of wagering, why won't they work for a higher level of wagering" ? Answer: It is true that at any level of wagering the outcome should be positive. This means profits should be obtained

however,

if your bankroll is limited (and we assume that it is),then in order to earn *more* than $12 to $24 per hour, you will attempt to make additional wagers per hour. Sometimes with higher levels of wagering. This means that you, as a player, ***CANNOT BE AS SELECTIVE*** with your timely wagers. *It also lowers your winning percentage wagers and will result in more losses.* Temptation and worn out intuitive wagers will result in the poor timing of wagers. Some will blame it on bad luck or "cold" DICE. I would blame it on GREED.

Be content earning $12 to $24 per hour. With this author's knowledge, especially with altering the DICE generated outcomes, only wagers at the lower levels permit me to feel comfortable. In reality, I do not consider it gambling. After all, three points are in our favor:

(1) Insurance Factor of 18 wins to 6 losses or a 3 to 1 insurance factor.

(2) Fifteen percent of possible disastrous 7's are by-passed by observing shooter's techniques.

(3) Piloting your own ship containing cargo of hourly profits (earnings) through treacherous waters full of reefs and sandbars (the ugly 7's). Pilots use up-to-date charts. You will also use current charts depicting the flow of ocean currents (your flow of numbers).

BEWARE OF OTHER CRAP SHOOTERS

This is a most important subject for the journey onward to earn $12 to $24 per hour in the stimulating 'Arena of CRAP Action'.

During an average one-hour of CRAP play, there will be approximately 130 to 140 numbers sired by those exhilarating jumpin' dominoes. Every 36 numbers will average 6 - 7's over the time you are at the CRAP Tables. This means approximately one-sixth of all the numbers generated will be a 7. They can appear rather frequently, generally on target, and rarely infrequently — but always averaging one-sixth of the numbers thrown .

Therefore we can expect 22 to 24 - 7's every hour of CRAP play. I have experienced bypassing at least three to four 7's per hour by watching the shooter's 'modus operandi'.

Some of the techniques border on superstition, others are based on facts. Superstition or not, these techniques are worthwhile and worked to my advantage, and should work for you also.

Avoid CRAP shooters who use the following techniques in tossing the DICE:

(1) Tosses the DICE into either of the front corners of the furthest wall. There is no logical or mathematical basis for this but this type shooter's technique breeds 7's.

(2) Tosses the DICE nonchalantly, as if with no interest in the outcome.

(3) Sharply tosses DICE into front wall.

(4) Shooter takes an inordinate amount of time in creating his specific pre-set of the DICE.

The above appears to have a superstitious approach, nevertheless my experiences warrants *"off all bets - no action"*.

Factually, there are various type DICE pre-sets that breed 7's. This is because the shooters pre-sets will alter the 36 Probability Table.

Please note carefully that under present conditions of tossing the DICE against the special padded front wall the DICE bounce back in all directions. The days of yore when we had sophisticated CRAP shooters who merely tossed the DICE against a flat wall, or on a flat surface generating desired numbers, are completely gone.

DICE mechanics are a thing of the past, but this is my theory regarding altering the outcome of tossed DIE.

I repeat, altering the 36 Probability or 36 Frequency Table is not a definite control of the DICE. By 'altering' the DICE it is meant - altering or changing the amount of a given number from its frequency pattern. Example would be having a specific pre-set of the DICE that would increase the amount of 7's per 36 numbers from 6 times to 8 or 9 times. This is an increase of 33 % to 50 % giving a tremendous advantage when shooting on the come out roll.

Back to basics. In the long term of playing time, it is suggested that when a shooter uses a pre-determined pre-set of the DICE that have a CRAP number on the top surfaces (2, 3, 12) then instruct the dealer IMMEDIATELY before the DICE leaves the shooter's hands: "NO ACTION." or "OFF ! ! !"

For this contract between you and the casino to be valid, the dealer must respond by repeating "No Action" or "Off".

The best way to handle this is to observe the shooter's 'modus-operandi' BEFORE making any wagers. Generally speaking, even though there is a continuous change in the players, the majority of players would be present during your period of play at a particular table. Again, observe and make your decision to wager in sufficient time, depending on your personal intuitive opinion regarding shooter's tossing techniques.

What does this do for you ? If you as a player can *avoid* three to four 7's in this manner per hour, then you have avoided approximately 15 % of the 7's that can financially hurt you .

CRAPS for the Place Bettor is really a guessing game. You are continuously attempting to obtain a ratio between wins and losses to net your $12 to $24 per hour.

When place betting the inside numbers for the smallest wagers at a $5 minimum wager table, you are exposing a $22 investment that can be LOST whenever the 7's develops.

Repeat: You will have winning wagers and losing wagers. Every win on an inside number (5, 6, 8, 9) will pay $7 each for the minimum wager. Each loss will cause you to lose all place bet wagers on the inside numbers.

For informational purposes, a breakeven win-loss ratio would be:

$$\text{Investment} = \$\ 22$$
$$\text{Win Pay-off} = \$\ 7$$

$$\text{Breakeven ratio} = \frac{\$\ 22}{\$\ 7} = 3.14\ (\text{Mathematics} = \text{Pi})$$

Translated this means, that in order to break-even, you would have to have 3.14 wins for every 1 loss.

Our goal is a minimum of 4 wins to every 1 loss. During a span of each hour, our goal would be a net win of $12 to $24. Not bad when you are having fun time and grinding the casinos for your earnings.

KEENLY OBSERVE PRE-SETS

On your path to earn $12 to $24 per hour, you will need every tool available to avoid that financially ruinous 7. It only takes one 7 to send your stack of place bet chips tumbling down, only to be reassembled in the dealer's collection.

Your knowledge of DICE mechanics is to permit you **not** to wager on the place bets when the shooter pre-sets the DICE on certain values (setting of the DICE).

When a CRAP shooter deliberately pre-sets the DICE on any seven (1-6, 2-5, 3-4) *do not* make any place bets.

If the pre-sets (top surfaces) are set on any CRAP number (2, 3, 12) *do not* make any place bets.

There will be exceptions, but in the long run you will be better off. After all, our goal is a **minimum** of four place bet wins to every losing 7 roll.

By observing the shooters 'modus-operandi' you will increase your chances of earning $12 to $24 per hour. Don't be upset if there are exceptions where the shooter's wins outweigh the one devilish 7 by factors exceeding five-to-one. In the final analysis, you will be earning your $12 to $24 per hour if you generally avoid certain DICE pre-sets.

You are probably wondering why the 11 pre-set was not included in this category ? Simple answer. Two of this authors pre-sets, for more place bet numbers than theoretically expected, have the pre-set value of 11 on the top two surfaces of the DICE. In addition the very two the longest shooter's rolls that I personally witnessed had the 11 on the top two surfaces.

Forget about using pre-sets to earn money as a shooter. It will not happen for a novice. There is more involved than can be briefly explained. Wait until you have six months of earnings under your belt, then if you want more fun time with additional earning potential, purchase my book on "DICE MECHANICS, CRAPS, HORNS, WHIRLS and HARDWAYS."

Don't attempt to be a shooter, especially while toying with pre-setting the DICE, unless you want to waste the price of this book, waste your time, and lose your bankroll. Worst of all, you would waste the opportunity to exist with profits through the recession ! ! !

CASINOS DEVOUR OVER
34 % OF CRAP BANKROLL

MISTAKEN IDENTIFICATION

The New Jersey Casino Commission together with all Atlantic City Casinos unwittingly erred in calculating the true Casino's win percentage for CRAPS,

The data obtained by the drop and win figures gives the commission a basis for reference. However, I state that the Casino's real win percentage is higher than published.

By simple arithmetic, we can show that there is a "duplication" of dollar drop. The Casino's dollar win divided by a lower correct dollar drop would result in a higher Casino win percentage in CRAPS.

Let's think about this for a moment.

Assume that a typical player exchanges $200 for chips. After playing CRAPS for two hours, lets suppose it may be time for lunch or dinner. The run-of-the-mill player goes to the cashier's cage and exchanges the chips for $80 or $280 in currency. Why carry around dirty, heavy chips when temporarily leaving the casino ?
After eating something light, the player returns to the CRAP Action Arena and exchanges possibly $100 or $200 for chips. Now what do we have ? If the player never exchanged chips for currency until the very end of play, be it at the end of one session, one day, one weekend, or as long as he or she is a player — then the dollar drop would be lower. Think about it !

Sometimes players will cash in their chips to change their luck.

I am certain that you as a reader can offer more times when chips are exchanged for currency:

>   Security Reasons
>   Snack Time
>   Fitness Room Visits
>   Swim Time
>   Massage Time
>   Rest Periods
>   Show Time
>   etc.

After talking with key casino executives, I find that it is a practice among some players with higher credit limits to ask for a sizable marker, possibly play for a short period of time and then leave the casino. In this manner the player has obtained an interest free loan.

Some casinos have a credit policy that markers for less than $500 are due in thirty days while markers exceeding $5000 have effectively interest-free time of 90 days.

One of the casinos top credit executives told me of a prominent Atlantic City businessman who obtained a marker for $25,000. Then proceeding immediately to the cashier's cage to cash-in. Thus easily securing an interest free "loan".

Apparently this is more common that I expected. I also was informed that many players frequently cash in their chips for fresh money. They hope to give the impression to the casino people that they are investing more money so they can obtain larger comps. These two examples certainly add to the false dollar drop figures, and according to top knowledgeable executives, the dollar drop is dramatically affected by these false dollar drops.

Information obtained from casino executives was encouraging. One source estimated this duplication at about 30 %. Six other sources stated it ranged from 20 % to 25 %. These estimates were in the proper direction, but low ! ! !

NEW JERSEY CASINO CONTROL COMMISSION RESULTS

1991 Recorded CRAPS Drop	=	$ 2,275,571,000
Casino's Dollar Win	=	$ 348,872,000
Casino's Win Percentage	=	15.33 %

AUTHOR'S EVALUATION

The average typical CRAP player's time would be one daily session.

During a four months period, I spoke to over four hundred players. These conversations took less than two minutes each. The following analysis was predicated on a typical 100 CRAP players.

Question:
> "Normally how many times during a day do you cash in your chips for any reason such as meal time showtime or breaktime ?"

Analysis:

Players	Extra trip to Cash In	False Drops
34	0	0
27	1	27
21	2	42
14	3	42
3	4	12
1	5	5
100		128

Let's assume, for simplicity, that these 100 typical CRAP players initially purchased $100 in chips. Now a break is needed. It may be that he or she may be down $30 to $40 or up possibly $20 to $80. It really does not matter. If player A is down $27 and received $73 for his or her chips, it is almost a certainty that upon returning to the casino another $100 will be tendered for chips. It also go to say that if player B won $61 and received $161 for the chips, it is again a certainty that he will also tender $100 for chips when re-entering the Arena of CRAP Action.

An area worth discussing is the larger player who has dedicated $1000 to $5000 as his CRAP bankroll. To obtain potential comps this player may tender this money or marker at the outset of play. But as time and DICE take their toll, the CRAP bankroll will continuously dwindle. Therefore after exchanging chips for paper currency or reduction of a marker, two things will occur. Most likely the **cash** player will tender less cash when returning to the tables. But the **marker type** character will again re-establish his comp potential by requesting the "full marker" as before.

I believe the overall difference in calculating the false drop is negligible. It is also my opinion that the bulk of drops are financed (yes, financed) by the smaller players.

So onward to our analysis.

According to our "typical 100 CRAP players" twenty-seven (27) made one additional trip to the cashiers cage besides the final trip at daily sessions end. This accounts for 27 false drops. Twenty-one (21) made two additional trips to exchange chips for currency. Obviously these 21 players account for 42 false drops. Going through the same process we have a total of 128 false drops.

Assuming this typical group each had initial drops of $100 and each following drop was of the same magnitude, we can arrive some interesting conclusions. Yes, I will admit that portions of the false drops will be less than players original drop. But according to my poll most players re-entered our invigorating arena of action with approximately the same CRAP bankroll.

Knowing this, let's proceed:

Original CRAP bankrolls = 100 players x $100 = $10,000
Extra (false) drops   = 128 x $100   = $12,800
                                                $22,800

Casino's win based on 100 % drop for 1991 = 15.33 %
          15.33 % of $22,800 = $3,495

$$\frac{\$3,495}{\text{Original } \$10,000} = 34.95 \quad \text{UGH ! ! !}$$

This is what the Casinos devour and consume
from the CRAP players bankroll ! ! !

This is no reflection on the casinos or the New Jersey Casino
Control Commission. There is no accurate method to exactly
measure the duplication of dollar drop. The information is
only presented to let the public know that the **Casino's True
Win Percentage On Craps Is Higher By Over 100% than
Indicated.**

DECREASING PERCENTAGES

What goofballs we have in the Arena of CRAP Action ! ! !

This includes most authors, most so-called CRAP experts, and almost everyone involved in the game of CRAPS. Including casino personnel (from top to bottom) and those CRAP playing math wizards.

They just never understood CRAPS. John Scarne laid the groundwork. Obviously no subsequent author ever fully and completely investigated the *odds aspect* of the game, until now.

Everyone of the previous CRAP authors state that the more odds a pass line player takes, or the more odds that a wrong bettor lays, the CRAP player's quality of play increases. This is because of the decreasing Casino's win percentage.

Imagine, all of these authorities never understanding CRAPS. It's sickening ! ! !

Look at the *decreasing percentages* as the pass line player *increases risk* money to reduce the Casino's win percentage in order to maintain a constant player's dollar loss or a constant Casino dollar win. The constant loss for the player will always be 248 times the dollar value of the pass line wager *once the point number is established.* In this case $5 times 248 or $1240 per the 1320 pass line points taken place during the 14 hours (1980 tosses of the DICE), assuming a $5 pass line wager.

DECREASING PERCENTAGES

$ 1240 PASS LINE LOSS
for every $5 pass line wager
(Once Point Number is Established)

For simplification:

In over 1980 numbers generated by those mystifying DICE, the pass line point **losers** (784) **exceed** the pass line point **winners** (536) by 248.

For every $5 bet on Pass Line and Come Bet (once the point number is established) over a period of 1320 point numbers, (total of losers and winners) the pass line bettor is expected to lose $1240.

$$248 \text{ more losers } \times \$5 \text{ each bet } = \$1240.$$

$$\frac{784 \text{ losers}}{1320 \text{ total point numbers}} = \mathbf{59.39 \%} \text{ Pass Line Point } \mathbf{Losers}$$

$$\frac{784 \text{ losers}}{536 \text{ winners}} = \begin{array}{l} 1.4627 \text{ or } 46.27 \% \textbf{ more } \text{Pass Line} \\ \text{Point Losers than Winners} \end{array}$$

Santa Claus for the Casino is the Pass Line and Don't Pass Line player.

DECREASING CASINO'S WIN PERCENTAGE BUT CONSTANT CASINO DOLLAR WIN

Novice players move on to the green pastures (*Place Bets*). Let's take time to prove to those *Doubting Thomases* that what I am saying about those stupid decreasing percentages, as they relate to the increased investment of odds, are true.

No Odds:
        Investment: = 1320 Points x $ 5 = $ 6,600
        Casino's win: 1,240
        Casino's percentage: 18.79 %

Single Odds:
        Investment: = 1320 Points x $ 10 = $ 13,200
        Casino's win: 1,240
        Casino's percentage: 9.39 %

Double Odds:
        Investment: = 1320 Points x $ 15 = $ 19,800
        Casino's win: 1,240
        Casino's percentage: 6.26 %

Triple Odds:
        Investment: = 1320 Points x $ 20 = $ 26,400
        Casino's win: 1,240
        Casino's percentage: 4.70 %

Five x Odds:
        Investment: = 1320 Points x $ 30 = $ 39,600
        Casino's win: 1,240
        Casino's percentage;   3.13 %

One Hundred x Odds:
        Investment: = 1320 Points x $505 = $666,600
        Casino's win: 1,240
        Casino's percentage: 0.186 %

SUMMARY:

For every dollar wager on the Pass Line, the casino expects to win 248 times this amount over the course of the 1320 pass line point numbers, once point number is established.

I admit that sometimes "hot streaks" appear. After reviewing my personal charts over the past ten years, they reveal that the pass line losers exceed the pass line winners by more than 69 %, instead of the expected 46 %. This fact appeared approximately 65 % of the time . The other 35 % of the time tends to balance the scale.

If you, as a player, are maximizing the "free odds" opportunity, you will be without funds very quickly. True the opposite can occur, but I have no scientific basis to say this but from historical experience, **it won't happen !**

WORTH REPEATING

Pass Line Percentages

Once the pass line point number is established, then, at this very instant, the casino's win percentage is 18.79 %. Not what most authorities believe it to be, 1.414 %. The reason they have the low 1.414 % is due to the tremendous two-to-one win factor during the Come Out Rolls. Over a time period (about 14 hours or 1980 tosses), assuming that the pass line player is always wagering on the come out roll, the pass line will lose 28 times more often than it wins. On the come-out-roll, the pass line wager will win 440 times while losing 220 times, as indicated on the1980 Probability Table. **This tremendous come-out-roll advantage breeds 220 net wins.**

Hell freezes over once the point number is established. From the 1980 Probability Table, there will be 1320 point numbers, of which 784 pass line point numbers are doomed for failure, and 536 pass line point numbers will succeed. This is why the pass line is a HORRENDOUS WAGER once the point number is established.

Pass Line Point Number Losses	784
Pass Line Point Number Wins	- 536
Net Point Number Losses	248
Net Come-Out-Roll Wins	- 220
Net Pass Line LOSSES	28

Hence the casino's overall win percentage for the pass line with no odds is:

$$\frac{28 \text{ Net Losses}}{1980 \text{ Total Numbers}} = 1.414 \text{ \%}$$

Note: At the instant that a pass line point number is established, the Casino's win percentage is 18.79 % _not_ 1.414 % as most players and experts believe.

The 18.79 % casino's win percentage is a weighted percentage.

Individually, the casino's win percentage is:

Point Number	Casino's Win Percentage
4 or 10	33.33 %
5 or 9	20.00 %
6 or 8	9.09 %

You can see why I must call the other authors unknowledgeable !

Note: $\dfrac{248 \text{ Pass Line Point Losers}}{1320 \text{ Point Numbers}} = 18.79 \%$

$$\frac{18.788 \%}{1.414 \%} = 13.3 \text{ times larger}$$

Another Method Of Calculating The
CASINO'S WIN PERCENTAGE
At The Instant The Pass Line Point Is Thrown

No Odds:

Investment: = Number of events x Wager

or

= 1320 events x $ 5 wager = $ 6600

Return: = Wins ($ 5 + $ 5 Return)

or

536 Pass Line Point Wins x $ 10 = $ 5360

Casino's win: $ 1240

Casino's Percentage: 18.79 %

When betting just on the pass line, with no place bets, the insurance factor decreases dramatically. This is another reason *I consider the Pass Line Bet a Horrendous Bet,* except for exciting fun and intuitive bets when pre-setting successfully. This type of betting is at least six months of experience down the income earning road.

Not One CRAP Author Ever Stated

"The Pass Line Wager Is A Bad Bet"
Or
"The Odds Wager Is A Terrible Wager"

Actually the other authors state that the pass line and don't pass line are the very best wagers with maximum odds taken or layed.

The "1980 Probability Table" was created because the number "1980" is the lowest common denominator to eliminate decimals and fractions (36 x 55 = 1980).

The 36 (6 x 6) is the total possible combinations of two DICE.

The number 55 is derived from the true odds of our six pass line point numbers:

Point Number	Odds
4 or 10	2/1
5 or 9	3/2
6 or 8	6/5

* This information indicates that 55 is the Lowest Common Denominator on: 1, 2, 3, 5, 6, and 11.

$$36 \times 55 = 1980$$

as the smallest number of tosses to eliminate decimals and fractions.

* 1, 2, 3 and 6 are eliminated because they divide into 36 wholly.

RESULTS of "FREE ODDS" AFTER PASS LINE NUMBER IS ESTABLISHED

Casino's Percentages

Numbers	No Odds	Single Odds	Double Odds	Five x Odds	Ten x Odds
4 or 10	33.3	16.7	11.1	5.56	3.03
5 or 9	20.0	***10.0	6.67	3.33	1.82
6 or 8	9.09	4.5	3.03	1.515	0.826

In all cases above the casino's dollar return remains constant per table below. This means that for the *total number of events* the Casino Dollar Return is a function of the Pass Line number.

* Events	Numbers	** Casino Dollar ($) Return
3 + 6 = 9	4 & 10	3 x Pass Line bet
4 + 6 = 10	5 & 9	2 x Pass Line bet.
5 + 6 = 11	6 & 8	1 x Pass Line bet

* Events = Ways to win PLUS ways to lose.

** For number of events

*** For Single Odds, 10.0 % is the correct Casino's percentage when the Pass Line bet equals the single odds bet. But if Pass Line bet is $5 and the odds bet is $6 the Casino's percentage decreases to 9.09 %. This is because the single odds wager is 20 % larger than the $5 Pass Line wager.

MATH ODDITY

Odds Multiple of Pass Line Wager	=	Casino's Win Percentage as related to Zero Odds	
Zero		1	18.79 %
Single		1/2	9.39 %
Double		1/3	6.26 %
*Triple		1/4	4.70 %
Five Times		1/6	3.13 %
One Hundred Times		1/101	0.186 %

Therefore as the value of the odds multiple increases, the Casino's Win Percentage will be:

$$\frac{18.79\%}{(\text{Multiple of Odds Plus One})}$$

* Example for triple odds $= \dfrac{18.79\%}{(3+1)} = 4.70\ \%$

REMEMBER:

These Are The Casino's Win Percentages
After
The Point Is Established

In honor of those Nevada Casinos that offer ten (10) times odds, what will be the Casino's Win Percentage using the math oddity shortcut ?

$$\frac{18.79\%}{10 + 1} = \frac{18.79\%}{11} = 1.71\ \%$$

We know the Pass Line bettor will *lose* in dollars 248 times the Pass Line wager, over a period of 1320 Pass Line point numbers. This is based on the condition that a wager is made on every one of the 1980 DICE tosses which will take approximately 14 hours.

Not One Crap Author Ever Stated That
"THE PASS LINE WAGER IS A BAD BET"
Or That
"THE ODDS WAGER IS A TERRIBLE WAGER"

EARNING CRAP PAYROLL MONEY

No deductions for taxes or fringe benefits will be made. The only deductions will be the running losses from your total winnings.

Zeke's Techniques will assist you in creating a minimum of four wins for every loss:

Winnings:	4 Wins x $ 7 =	$ 28
Loss:	1 Loss =	22
	Net Win: =	$ 6

Your minimum goal should be earnings $12 per hour. This relates to only **two losses** per **eight wins**. This also relates to ten decisions per hour once the point number is established.

It's a nice, easy-going pace, and should be enjoyable especially while you are winning. Winning however, is only a temporary situation. The table can be cold but you can still be a winner.

By using Zeke's techniques, this minimum earning achievement should be accomplished. Keep in mind these important steps:

Being Patient
Avoiding Greed
Use Charting Technique
Wagering On Place Bets Only
Never Press Place bets

If an increase in Place bet wagers is desired, and appears timely as reflected by charting, **wait until a new shooter.** Only increase Place bets to next level after a win. If Place betting the inside numbers (5, 6, 8, 9) it is suggested that only the 6 and 8 be increased to next level only. Do this until accustomed to higher value of risk. Instead of a $22 exposure on the inside numbers (5, 6, 8, 9), the exposure would increase to $34. *After a win remove all Place bets.*

If chart approved and comfortably ahead of your goal of $12 to $24 per hour, go for the second hit in the following manner. A win occurring on the 6 and 8 would indicate *remove all Place bets except* ($6) *wagers on the 6 and 8.* Should a 7 erupt before a second win, you would have won $14 and lost $12, or a net win of $2. Another win on the 6 and 8 would be a net win of $21 on this shooter.

Should the first win on this new shooter be the 5 or 9, *remove the 5 and 9* but leave $6 each on the 6 and 8. This is done by instructing the dealer: "Down on the 5 and 9 and leave $6 each on the 6 and 8 for a total of $12."

Should a 5 or 9 reappear again tell the dealer: "Down on everything."

This technique is superb when chart approved and comfortably ahead of hourly goal of $12 to $24.

ZEKE'S TECHNIQUES

1. For earning an income of $12 to $24 per hour *only* wager on the place bets.

2. *Never press Place bets*

3. Best bet would be one hit (win) and complete removal of all place bets, preferably the inside numbers of 5, 6, 8 and 9. Then wait for new shooter for next wager.

4. Add insurance factor by charting.

5. Add additional insurance by super-charting. Super-charting is the compiling and comparing the total number of 7's to the total numbers rolled (including 7's). Theoretically, the 7's should be one-sixth of the total numbers.

6. Mega-charting adds an important flavor of insurance. Mega-charting is keeping a running total of inside numbers (5, 6, 8, 9) as compared to total numbers generated. Mega-charting is only effective when Super-charting indicates that future rolls could be low in 7's. Inside numbers (5, 6, 8, 9) theoretically should be one-half of total numbers.

7. Increase value of place bets only after win at beginning of new shooter, when suggested by Chart, Super-chart and Mega-chart.

8. **Never play Pass Line unless shooting DICE.** When shooting

(as in fun time, etc.) place at least three place bets. If equipped with proper pre-set, then possibly go for two or more wins. As a novice income earner, you are six months away.

9. Avoid proposition bets except for fun time, pre-set time and intuitive time. Also six months away.

10. Five place bets when chart approved are superb bets. Be careful about second or more wins. Suggest removal of first hit place bet, then remove each successive win. If removed bets are generated again then remove balance of place bets. Financial risk is greater than normal, be very very careful. Only place five wagers when ahead ! ! !

11. Historical charting shows that if place bet is not won within a given number of tosses, it is wise to remove all place bets. This given number can range from five to seven depending upon charting and intuitive feeling. Given numbers include every number from beginning of roll, including numbers before establishing point number.

12. There is no scientific reason for this, but if first three numbers of new shooter are craps, sevens or elevens (any combination) this author has gained by not making any Place bets. My personal records for the past 15 years indicate that the odds against any point number being made exceeds 5 to 1. Now you know this should not be the case, but for me it works.

13. Omitted for superstitious reasons.

14. Place bets on all six numbers (4, 5, 6, 8, 9 AND 10) are superior bets for one, two, and three possible hits when chart approved. Suggest removal of place bets that are won. If removed place bet is hit again, then remove remaining place bets. Intuition and charting should help in decision. **Very risky, even for the experienced player.** It is preferred to opt for two wins on the four inside numbers (5, 6, 8, 9).

15. When place bets have higher dollar value than your normal wager and you are attempting a second win, **it is strongly suggested** that you reduce dollar amount for second attempt. Also remove place bet that is won, or at least reduce dollar value on winning place bet.

16. **Remove all Place wagers if any of the following occurs:**
   (1) One or both dice leave the CRAP table.
   (2) The shooter drops one DIE or both DICE.
   (3) A new stickperson replaces the previous stickperson.
   (4) The shooter throws the DICE nonchalantly with no sincerity.
   (5) The shooter changes one or both DICE.
   (6) The shooter whips DICE with much more than normal force against back wall.
   (7) Shooter aims for either corner of back wall.
   (8) Any time that player feels intuitively that the ugly seven is due.

17. Pass Line betting time. (Six Months Later)
   (a) Fun Time
   (b) Superstitious Time
   (c) Intuitive Time

18. **Never** chase a consecutive series of shooter's losing rolls without any inside numbers (5, 6, 8 and 9) appearing before the ugly seven, after new point number is established.

19. **Never** increase Place bets after a loss.

20. **Never** make Place bets in the middle of an unknown roll.

21. When properly increasing dollar value of place bets, chart and intuition may suggest increasing certain place bets selectively above basic increase. Definitely when any of these numbers are hit and won, remove this number completely and again reduce dollar value of other place bets. Sometimes I benefit leaving wagers on the 6 AND 8, no matter if one of these was hit already.

22. **Never** work Place bets on the come out roll.

23. **Never** wager on the family of Don't Pass Bets and Don't Come Bets.

24. **Never** wager on the family of Pass Line Bets and Come Bets. When you are a shooter, play Pass Line but **no** Come bets. Taking odds is a preference of Pre-set and intuition. (Six months later, after comfortably earning an income).

25. An excellent technique when playing the inside place bets on the 5, 6, 8 and 9; if 5 or 9 is made (won) then remove

both the 5 & 9 and let the 6 & 8 remain. If the 6 **or** 8 is hit then remove **both** the 6 and 8. **IMPORTANT:** If 5 or 9 is repeated again, remove **both** the 6 and 8.

26. **Avoid** Place bets on the 4 or 10. Even when chart approved and good intuitive feeling, it is a gamble - a very low percentage of earning any income.

VERY IMPORTANT:

Whenever you approach ANY CRAP TABLE, chart and observe the numbers generated by the DICE for at least 10 minutes. This would be a minimum of 22 numbers.

HORRENDOUS WAGERS ! ! !

- Pass Line
- Don't Pass Line
- Come Bet
- Don't Come Bet
- Vigorish to Buy 4 or 10
- Place Bets 4 or 10
- Odds Behind Pass Line
- Laying Odds for Wrong Bettor
- Pressing *Any* Place Bets

The above imbecilic stupid CRAP play accounts for over 92 % of the casino's dollar win at CRAPS.

Casino CRAPS cannot be BEAT as suggested by *other authors, so called crap experts* or *gambling authorities.*

Please explain to me why there are less than one percent overall CRAP winners. Could it be because every book written on how to win at CRAPS or Beat the Casino repeats the same smelly garbage? Some attempt cute-sy plays, and others try money management. When, in the final analysis the success rate winning at CRAPS is less than one percent. And these winners did not learn anything from the "experts". They combined street-sense with common sense to become self-taught.

You should be angry, embittered and disgusted that you followed the CRAP cowpath of previous players and authors. A winning success rate of only one percent (and those were probably SELF-TAUGHT) suggested *pit-falls* with other playing methods.

I am also irritated. Education, in any subject matter, should enable you to go further in life to newer heights — *not* directing you to the FINANCIAL SEWER ! ! !

Today, the success rate for winners in the Arena of CRAP Action is LESS than one (1%) percent.

The success rate of my readers should greatly exceed twenty (20 %) percent. This rate is more than twenty times greater than present day winners.

Failures will result *not* because of the call of the wild (stickman's call), but because people are basically *greedy.* They want one more place bet win, sometimes after a full press. Or they *lack patience.* Combined, these faults will exist because of *no self discipline.*

This twenty-plus percent success rate could be much higher. High enough to force the luxurious casinos to change CRAP odds in order to continue making a profit in the Hippodrome of CRAP Action.

The rate of CRAP success will not increase because of human nature:

GREED

LACK OF PATIENCE

LACK OF DISCIPLINE

Even those that fail will recognize it was not because of the call of the wild (stickman's call of the DICE numbers generated). Honest thinking losers will admittedly blame themselves in disgust. Some will retrench and go back to basics, most will not ! ! !

THIS IS WHY PLACE BETTORS ARE LOSERS !

Two Wins Are More Profitable Than Five Wins
Two Wins Are Better Than Six Wins

This is very intriguing. There is a mathematical basis for making such a statement. Let's first assume using the four inside numbers (5, 6, 8, 9), each with the minimum wager ($22 total), we have been on target chart-wise and have recorded two wins so far. At the point of the second win, the profit for this shooter is two times $7 or $14.

If we now remove our four inside wagers, our $14 profit for this shooter is clearly protected. Let's project into the future what would happen if we permitted our $22 investment to remain as we go for broke:

Win #	Profit Including This Win	Net Income if 7 Before next Win	
3	$ 21	Loss	$ 1
4	$ 28	Profit	$ 6
5	$ 35	Profit	$ 13
6	$ 42	Profit	$ 20

This projection should help us take a positive posture. The most serious decision a CRAP player has when he is pressing his place bets is *when should he completely remove or decrease dollar value of Press Bets.* This is really a dilemma ! !

Let's relate this to the fortunate income earner ($12 to $24 per hour) who has two wins for a $14 profit if the inside (5, 6, 8, 9) place bets are removed.

This is clearly the only decision our income earner can make if the goal is to become a consistent income earner.

Be content with two wins, a profit of $14. If greedy for the elusive long inside number rich roll, after three additional wins on the inside numbers (5, 6, 8, 9) and then a loss of $22, the profit would have decreased to $13. Going for four additional wins profit will increase from $14 to $20 if a destructive seven then appears.

I repeat - going for three additional wins (total of five) and then the 7's pops up. This reduces the $14 profit to $13.

Four additional wins, and then a non-removal of place bets, results in a total profit for this shooter of $20 when the 7 appears.

Good gosh ! Five wins for less profit than two wins ($13 instead of $14).

Gosh by golly ! Six total wins (or four wins more than two wins) increases profits from $14 to $20. But you must travel through hell avoiding 7's for four additional wins for a mere increase of only $6.

You make this simple decision. Same dilemma as the Place Bet Presser. *When do you remove the place bets or decrease risk ?*

My solution: Go easy. The casino wants you to give them time with the action so they can tempt you with comps. These comps will grind you down and out. Obviously you want to grind the Casino for your just reward ($12 to $24 per hour).

This analysis is very basic and simple. Never before disclosed or discussed by any previous author. It is just an added event why there are less than 1 % overall winners in the exhilarating Hippodrome of CRAP Action.

WHEN PLACE BETTING ALL SIX NUMBERS

TWO WINS ARE MORE PROFITABLE THAN SIX WINS

AND BETTER THAN SEVEN WINS

Let's find out:

TWO HITS (WINS) ARE BETTER THAN SIX WINS ?

Win #	Profit Including This Win	Net Income of 7 Before next Win
1	$ 7.50	Loss $ 24.50
2	$ 15.00	Loss $ 17.00
3	$ 22.50	Loss $ 9.50
4	$ 30.00	Loss $ 2.00
5	$ 37.50	Win $ 5.50
6	$ 45.00	Win $ 13.00
7	$ 52.50	Win $ 20.50

Let's analyze the above chart.

The dilemma of the CRAP player ! ! !

When, oh when, should we remove our Place Bets ?

Two Wins Are Best

Place Bet Number	4	5	6	8	9	10		
Investment ($)	5	5	6	6	5	5	=	32
Pay-off ($)	9	7	7	7	7	9		
Ways to Win	3	4	5	5	4	3	=	24
Total Pay-off ($)	27	28	35	35	28	27	=	180

$$\text{Average Pay-off} = \frac{\$180}{24} = \$7.50$$

Let's project into the future. After how many wins is it wise to remove all six Place bets ?

The answer is very obvious. Enjoy two wins for a $ 15 profit and **then remove all Place bets.** Now we have protected the $ 15 profit for this shooter. Going for broke, after four more wins (making a total of six wins), only gives you a net win of $ 13. This is $ 2 LESS than only two wins. Can this be ? Let me say it again: going for broke, or letting the six place bets (4, 5, 6, 8, 9, 10) remain active until the deadly singular 7 shows up, is not a good idea. We are much better off with two wins than six wins. In fact, if the Gods Of Fate would favor us with seven wins, our net gain would only be $20.50 or $5.50 more than only two wins.

Soon to be published is my book on "Casino CRAPS — Probabilities and Odds", which contains some really fascinating information.

Without delving into derivations, allow me merely to present certain facts about the probability of two wins, six wins and seven wins for the six place bets (4, 5, 6, 8, 9,10).

* Number of Wins	Probability	Odds to Win	Odds Against Winning
2	0.64000	** 1.78	
6	0.26214		** 2.81
7	0.20972		3.77

* Before the fatal seven.
** Odds to one.

Besides the practicality of earning more with two wins than with six wins on our six place bets, another sound reason for two wins rather than six or seven wins is found when analyzing the results of the probabilities of these wins. The probabilities of two wins, six wins and seven wins converts into the odds of making two wins and the odds against making six and seven wins.

It's great knowing the odds of winning two times on the six Place bets is in our favor (1.78 to 1), but the odds against six wins are 2.81 **against** our favor. For seven wins the odds **against** this occurring are 3.77 to 1.

**This is one of the reasons why CRAP players
end up in the financial CRAP-per.**

Allow me to digress. Almost 18 months ago, when I began compiling articles about this very fascinating game of CRAPS, I learned some interesting facts. One of my first new disclosures was that by combining various place bets the casino's win percentages decreased dramatically. To obtain an opinion how the unknowing gambling public, authors and CRAP experts would react to my new findings, I presented my calculations to one of the most renowned casino executives. He brought along an expert on various table games, especially CRAPS. After reviewing my presentation, they both agreed: "Zeke, these are only numbers. What do numbers have to do with those crazy DICE ?"

I REST MY CASE.

IMPORTANT TABLES

36 PROBABILITY TABLE

Number	Possibilities
2	1
3	2
4	3
5	4
6	5
7	6
8	5
9	4
10	3
11	2
12	1

36 COMBINATIONS

Two Six Sided Cubes Can Generate
36 Different Combinations of Numbers

From the 36 Probability Table we create the 1980 Probability by multiplying 36 x 55 to obtain 1980. This is the smallest number to obtain the various **Casino's win percentages** on every possible CRAP wager without using fractions.

Right Bettor's 1980 Probability Table

Come Out Rolls	Winners	Losers
Eleven (11)	110	
Seven (7)	330	
Two (2)		55
Three (3)		110
Twelve (12)		55

Come Out Rolls = 440 + 220 = 660

Point Numbers

Point Numbers	Winners	Losers
Four (4)	55	110
Ten (10)	55	110
Five (5)	88	132
Nine (9)	88	132
Six (6)	125	150
Eight (8)	125	150

Points = 536 + 784 = 1320

1980

Total Losses = 220 + 784 = 1004
Total Wins = 440 + 536 = 976

Excess Losses = 28

$\frac{28}{1980}$ = 1.414% **Casino's win percentage** for Pass Line and Come Bet wagers

Wrong Bettor's 1980 Probability Table

Come Out Rolls	Winners	Losers
Eleven (11)		110
Seven (7)		330
Two (2)	55	
Three (3)	110	
*Twelve (12)	*Stand-off*	

Come Out Rolls = 165 + 440 = 605

Point Number

		Winners	Losers
Four	(4)	110	55
Ten	(10)	110	55
Five	(5)	132	88
Nine	(9)	132	88
Six	(6)	150	125
Eight	(8)	150	125

Points = 784 + 536 = 1320

1925 *

Total Losses = 440 + 536 = 976
Total Wins   = 165 + 784 = 949

Excess Losses = 27

$$\frac{27}{1925} = 1.40259 \%$$ **Casino's win percentage** for Don't Pass Line and Don't Come wagers

* (1980) - 55 for standoff #12 = 1925 *

CRAPS

ZEKE'S BEST BETS

Place Bets	Casino's %	Players Insurance Factor (wins / losses)
6-8	1.042	1.67
* 5-6-8-9	1.136	3.00
5-6-8	1.176	2.33
9-6-8	1.176	2.33
** 5-6-8-9	1.181	3.00
*** 4-5-6-8-9-10	1.250	4.00
**** 4-5-6-8-9-10	1.296	4.00
5-6-9	1.645	2.17
5-8-9	1.645	2.17

* When wagers are multiples of $ 22 total for all inside numbers

** When wagers are multiples of $ 30 for each of the inside numbers

*** When wagers are multiples of $ 32 total for all numbers

**** When wagers are multiples of $ 30 for each of the numbers

REMOVE ALL PLACE BETS AFTER (1) WIN

CASINO'S ADVANTAGE ON EVERY POSSIBLE INDIVIDUAL CRAP BET

	Casino's Percentage
Don't Pass w D-Odds	0.459 %
Pass w D-Odds	0.606
Don't Pass w S-Odds	0.691
Don't Come w S-Odds	0.691
Pass w S-Odds	0.848
Come w S-Odds	0.848
Don't Pass	1.403
Pass	1.414
Don't Come	1.403
Come	1.414
Place Bet 6	1.515
Place Bet 8	1.515
Field, db. 2; trpl.12	2.78
Place Bet 5	4.00
Place Bet 9	4.00
Field, db. 2; dbl.12	5.56
Place Bet 4	6.67
Place Bet 10	6.67
Six	9.09
Eight	9.09
Hardway 6	9.09
Hardway 8	9.09
Hardway 4	11.11
Hardway 10	11.11

Any Crap	11.11
Eleven (16 for 1)	11.11
Three (16 for 1)	11.11
Two (31 for 1)	13.89
Twelve (31 for 1)	13.89
Eleven (15 for 1)	16.67
Three (15 for 1)	16.67
Two (30 for 1)	16.67
Twelve (30 for 1)	16.67
Seven (5 for 1)	16.67
Under 7 (1 for 1)	16.67
Over 7 (1 for 1)	16.67

All of these percentages are without the benefit of Zeke's Techniques

PASS LINE WAGERS VERSUS PLACE BETS

Compare the following casino's win percentages *once point number is established.*

WAGER		CASINO'S WIN PERCENTAGE%	
Inside Place Bets (5, 6, 8, 9)		1.136	
Pass Line Wager	(weighted)	18.79	No Odds
Pass Line Wager	(4 or 10)	33.33	No Odds
Pass Line Wager	(5 or 9)	20.00	No Odds
Pass Line Wager	(6 or 8)	9.09	No Odds
Pass Line Wager	(4 or 10)	16.7	Single Odds
* Pass Line Wager	(5 or 9)	10.00	Single Odds
** Pass Line Wager	(5 or 9)	9.09	Single Odds
Pass Line Wager	(6 or 8)	4.5	Single Odds
Pass Line Wager	(4 or 10)	11.1	Double Odds
Pass Line Wager	(5 or 9)	6.7	Double Odds
Pass Line Wager	(6 or 8)	3.03	Double Odds

* When Single Odds have equivalent wager as pass line

** When Single Odds are $6 and pass line wager = $ 5

YOUR ATTENTION, PLEASE ! ! !

NEVER CHASE A LOSING SERIES OF PLACE BETS BY INCREASING DOLLAR VALUES OF PLACE BETS. ONLY GAMBLING FOOLS WOULD INCREASE BASIC WAGERS BY FACTORS OF TWO, THREE OR FOUR TIMES. THIS WILL LEAD TO FINANCIAL DISASTER AND RUINATION.

REMEMBER THE CASINO GRINDS THE PLAYERS OUT OF THE GAME. LET'S GRIND THE CASINO FOR A PLEASURABLE INCOME ($12 to $24 PER HOUR).

LET ME MAKE THIS VERY CLEAR -
AFTER A LOSS, DO NOT MAKE ANY PLACE BETS UNTIL NEW SHOOTER GENERATES A 5, 6, 8 OR 9, AND THEN ONLY AFTER A NEW POINT NUMBER IS DECLARED. THEN, AND ONLY THEN, MAKE YOUR PLACE BETS.

THIS WILL AVOID THOSE TYPICAL AND NOT TOO RARE LOSSES: POINT, SEVEN — POINT, SEVEN — POINT, SEVEN. THIS IS ONE OF MY BEST TECHNIQUES. IT HAS SAVED ME OODLES OF LOSSES. IF THE DICE HAVE BEEN EXCESSIVELY COLD, ONLY PLACE THE 6 AND 8, IRRESPECTIVE OF POINT NUMBER.

WHAT TO DO ?

My practice of play is to win one place bet and then **remove all bets.** Sometimes I will remain for two wins before removing. I try to never let my Place bets remain for the entire roll of the shooter. Even when I am the shooter.

There have been occasions when the mannerisms of a shooter are to my choosing and I may go for three wins. So far I have been more lucky than smart.

Don't try to recoup unexpected losses in one or two larger than normal wagers.

The Casinos want time to grind you down and out ! ! !

Zeke's techniques gives you the skills to do to the casinos what they want to do to you. Only this time, you get the profits and pleasures.

HASTE MAKES WASTE

AVOID THE UNWANTED 7

I ALWAYS AVOID SHOOTERS TOSSING THE DICE AT AN
ANGLE INTO THE CORNERS

Don't ask me why, but it seems that the 7 appears more
frequently with this type shooter.

CORNER SHOOTING

This item is worth repeating. Over the years I have noticed that certain conditions breeds more than their share of 7's. During the past twelve months, I increased my notations regarding some of these conditions. Sometimes, while glance watching various sporting events, I review my notations. I can't explain it or the reasons it happens, but there is data for me to ponder.

Let's review my analysis.

(1)   Shooters who constantly toss the DICE for the corners, or a particular corner have the rarest of rare hot streaks. Instead of generating 7's every sixth toss (on the average), the rate of 7's thrown *increases* up to an additional 40 %.

(2)   These corner shooters who *whip* the DICE quickly and sharply into the corners on every toss add another factor causing the 7 to *increase* up to 50 % more often. No explanation, but true.

(3)   If a shooter in the middle of a roll suddenly aims the next toss into a corner, the probability that a 7 will develop is higher than the one out of six ratio. No explanation, only experience.

(4)   Should any of the above be combined with the ingredient of a new stickperson or component like DD (dropped DICE) or OT (off table) then the 7 is surely the deadly fling of the DICE.

As an engineer and amateur mathematician, I understand my documented results are not scientifically acknowledged, but, in my superstitious world, they work for me. Perhaps other "conditions" may work for you, but if you are playing at the same table it will work for you.

I am NOT INTO HOROSCOPES, PHRENOLOGY, PHYLACTERY, VOODOOISM, etc.

BUT

What counts is that it works for me, maybe for others.

CONVERSELY

The identical procreation of SEVENS is the resultant of a dispassionate, apathetic molder of numbers, the unconcerned nonchalant shooter

Simply - it works for me.

Warning - there are always exceptions, but they are unusual.

AVOID THE
UNWANTED SEVEN

INTUITION

**At anytime you feel uneasy about any condition,
remove your bets ! ! !**

DON'T BE GREEDY

NEVER PRESS PLACE BETS!

Increase values of Place bets at outset - when predicted by charting or super-charting.

USEFUL TIPS FOR
AVOIDING THE SEVEN (7)

Some may call it the dramatic instance, but I call it intuitive good luck. Definitely, it has been to my advantage to remove all place bets whenever there is an unusual delay in the game for any reason.

Mathematically and logically it has no explanation, but delays, the dark corner shots, changing of the stickperson and the DICE leaving the CRAP Table indicate that a sneaky, tricky seven is quickly due.

ONWARD TO YOUR GOAL OF $12 TO $24 PER HOUR.

INGREDIENTS REQUIRED TO EARN
$12 to $24 PER HOUR
WHILE ENJOYING FASCINATING
CASINO CRAPS

Patience

Lack of Greed

Charting Pad and Pen

Superstition

Zeke's Techniques

Bankroll minimum of $ 600

Beware ot the
Ugly 7

AUTHOR'S GLOSSARY

Free Odds	Really not so free. Suggest avoiding Death Trap.
Point Number	Pass Line number. A born loser. 50 % more Losers to Winners.
Place Bet Presser	One who is committing financial suicide.
Hardways	Good bet for three occasions:
	(a) Toke for Dealers
	(b) Fun Bet
	(c) Pre-Set Action
	—
Pass Line Bettor	Only for fun time, pre-sets, superstitious and intuitive times.
Wrong Bettor	One who believes he is smarter than pass line bettors.
Superstitious Bets	Scientifically brilliant.
Charting	Ruination of Casinos
CRAPS	Superb game for exhilaration, intrigue, fun and EARNINGS after you thoroughly understand this book.
HOT Streak	That most rare dream

Cold Streak	Many losing short rolls,
Long Roll	Great Luck. Mathematically very rare.
Short Roll	Not so great luck, but expected
36 Combination Table	The Gospel
1980 Combination Table	The BIBLE of CRAPS
Place Bets	**Only way** to earn $12 to $24 per hour.
Casino's %	Opulent environment, very high overhead and very high interest on junk bonds.
COMPS	Devious system to make gamblers pay for their own expenses.
Insurance	Combining Place Bets
Seven	Four ways for the Place bettor to overcome: (1) Avoidance (2) Superstition (3) Insurance (4) Watch other shooter's pre-sets
Tokes	Method of showing appreciation to dealers. Also necessary to offset

	low pay scales. Place directly into toke box.
"No Roll" Call	Area of confusion for New Jersey Casino Commission and Casinos
Drop	Money exchanged for chips at various table games by the unknowledgeable.
OT "Off Table"	All bets off!
DD - Dropped "DIE or DICE"	All bets off!
NS - New Stick Person	All bets off!
CRAPS Mathematics	Simple basic uncomplicated arithmetic
Casino Employment	Place to go to work and forget ambitious thoughts. Early retirement from a productive life.
Proposition Bets	Fun time bets only, unless skilled pre-setter. When played exclusively and extensively, it can confuse stickmen and box people.
Combining Place Bets	"God Bless America" and the really smart CRAP players.
Unknown Curse	"DICE" have no memory and every toss or roll of the DICE is

	completely independent of any previous toss of the DICE".
Pre-sets	Fun and Earning Income time.
Juice	Casino power play to insure hiring people with much less ability so as not to threaten his boss's position.
Casino Commission	Organization setup to divert attention from their inefficiencies and excessive expenditures by highlighting Donald Trump's possible financial problems. Goal - perpetual inactivity.
Pass Line Player	Afflicted with *WOE

*A condition of deep suffering from misfortune or grief.

CRAPS Terminology

Right Bettor: Wagers on Pass Line. Once point number is established, bettor is wagering point number will appear before the 7.

Wrong Bettor: Wagers that a 7 will appear before the point number Players have misconception that wagering as wrong bettor is the same as playing with the "house" or Casino.

Odds: Wagers taken or layed for the point numbers are paid at the true odds that the point will be made or not made. The expression of "true odds" is misleading. See "Decreasing Percentages".

Single Odds: Odds taken or layed are equal to line wager (or equivalent value in case of point number 5 or 9).

Double Odds: Odds taken or layed are equal to double the line wager.

Point Number: Shooter's point number is the very first 4, 5, 6, 8, 9 or 10 that appears on the come out roll, not including any CRAP numbers, 7's or 11's.

Place Bet: The place bet numbers can be 4, 5, 6, 8, 9 or 10. You can wager it will or will not appear before the next 7.

Pre-Set: Some CRAP players prepare for shooting the DICE with a pre-determined number setting on the top surfaces. Others also additionally pre-determine certain vertical surface number values. Generally this is a superstitious, ritual or prayer-like act.

The following gambling data for Atlantic City's Twelve Casinos was obtained from the New Jersey Casino Control Commission.

Special thanks to Carol Kokotajlo, Tom Flynn and Mike Pollack.

Bally's Grand
for the month of January, 1992

Casino Revenues	Authorized Units	Win	Drop	Win Percentage
Table Game				
Blackjack	58	2,803,255	18,090,491	15.5 %
Craps	18	1,817,335	11,382,337	16.0 %
Roulette	10	693,907	2,630,730	26.4 %
Big Six	3	83,121	187,697	44.3 %
Baccarat	2	274,191	2,306,284	11.9 %
Minibaccarat	2	139,292	917,434	15.2 %
Other (Red Dog & Sic Bo)	3	110,755	271,083	40.9 %
Total - Table Games	**96**	**5,921,856**	**35,786,056**	**16.5 %**
			Handle	
Coin Oper Machines				
$ .05 Slot Machines	69	229,129	1,591,113	14.4 %
$ .25 Slot Machines	464	2,081,069	15,679,027	13.3 %
$1.00 Slot Machines	167	1,479,172	14,795,025	10.0 %
Other Slot Machines	663	4,849,019	55,797,427	8.7 %
Total - Coin Oper. Machines	**1363**	**8,638,389**	**87,862,592**	**9.8 %**
Total Casino Revenues		**$ 14,560,245**		

Bally's Park Place
for the month of January, 1992

Casino Revenues	Authorized Units	Win	Drop	Win Percentage
Table Game				
Blackjack	70	2,811,320	21,406,167	13.1 %
Craps	18	1,892,518	9,528,428	19.9 %
Roulette	12	874,493	3,486,888	25.1 %
Big Six	4	158,563	364,097	43.6 %
Baccarat	2	273,049	2,094,579	13.0 %
Minibaccarat	2	224,848	1,441,920	15.6 %
Other (Red Dog & Sic Bo)	2	132,783	311,291	42.7 %
Total - Table Games	**110**	**6,367,574**	**38,633,366**	**16.5 %**
			Handle	
Coin Oper Machines				
$ .05 Slot Machines	92	327,593	1,978,742	16.6 %
$ .25 Slot Machines	675	2,996,963	23,559,262	12.7 %
$1.00 Slot Machines	229	2,576,138	26,806,813	9.6 %
Other Slot Machines	807	5,744,885	64,406,708	8.9 %
Total - Coin Oper. Machines	**1803**	**11,645,579**	**116,751,525**	**10.0 %**
Total Casino Revenues		**$ 18,013,153**		

Page 195

Caesars Atlantic City
for the month of January, 1992

Casino Revenues	Authorized Units	Win	Drop	Win Percentage
Table Game				
Blackjack	52	4,750,289	28,818,505	16.5 %
Craps	20	4,415,727	22,762,535	19.4 %
Roulette	13	1,070,875	5,379,564	19.9 %
Big Six	2	132,444	304,062	43.6 %
Baccarat	3	4,454,889	13,365,714	33.6 %
Minibaccarat	2	330,759	1,848,275	17.9 %
Other (Red Dog & Sic Bo)	2	146,644	403,947	36.3 %
Total - Table Games	94	15,301,627	72,782,602	21.0 %
			Handle	
Coin Oper Machines				
$ .05 Slot Machines	91	276,986	1,788,630	15.5 %
$ .25 Slot Machines	558	2,945,258	20,966,857	14.0 %
$1.00 Slot Machines	327	2,894,699	32,934,192	8.8 %
Other Slot Machines	835	6,570,371	73,424,620	8.9 %
Total - Coin Oper. Machines	1809	12,687,314	129,114,299	9.8 %
Total Casino Revenues		$ 27,988,941		

Page 196

Claridge Hotel & Casino
for the month of January, 1992

Casino Revenues	Authorized Units	Win	Drop	Win Percentage
Table Game				
Blackjack	45	1,621,348	11,750,517	13.8 %
Craps	10	1,191,036	7,521,319	15.8 %
Roulette	6	364,464	1,426,729	25.5 %
Big Six	1	53,628	124,017	43.2 %
Baccarat	1	(35,378)	195,063	18.1 %
Minibaccarat	1	40,446	448,775	9.0 %
Other (Red Dog & Sic Bo)	1	52,307	133,858	39.1 %
Total - Table Games	**65**	**3,287,851**	**21,600,278**	**15.2 %**
			Handle	
Coin Oper Machines				
$ .05 Slot Machines	69	176,927	1,151,383	15.4 %
$ .25 Slot Machines	410	2,169,874	16,754,151	13.0 %
$1.00 Slot Machines	217	1,166,077	10,887,210	10.7 %
Other Slot Machines	673	3,248,523	32,410,627	10.0 %
Total - Coin Oper. Machines	**1369**	**6,761,401**	**61,203,371**	**11.0 %**
Total Casino Revenues		**$ 10,049,252**		

Harrah's Casino Hotel
for the month of January, 1992

Casino Revenues	Authorized Units	Win	Drop	Win Percentage
Table Game				
Blackjack	45	1,621,348	11,750,517	13.8 %
Craps	10	1,191,036	7,521,319	15.8 %
Roulette	6	364,464	1,426,729	25.5 %
Big Six	1	53,628	124,017	43.2 %
Baccarat	1	(35,378)	195,063	-18.1 %
Minibaccarat	1	40,446	448,775	9.0 %
Other (Red Dog & Sic Bo)	1	52,307	133,858	39.1 %
Total - Table Games	65	3,287,851	21,600,278	15.2 %
			Handle	
Coin Oper Machines				
$ .05 Slot Machines	69	176,927	1,151,383	15.4 %
$ .25 Slot Machines	410	2,169,874	16,754,151	13.0 %
$1.00 Slot Machines	217	1,166,077	10,887,210	10.7 %
Other Slot Machines	673	3,248,523	32,410,627	10.0 %
Total - Coin Oper. Machines	1369	6,761,401	61,203,371	11.0 %
Total Casino Revenues		$ 10,049,252		

Page 198

Merv Griffin's Resort
for the month of January, 1992

Casino Revenues	Authorized Units	Win	Drop	Win Percentage
Table Game				
Blackjack	60	3,206,228	21,125,102	15.2 %
Craps	16	2,396,369	15,678,917	15.3 %
Roulette	13	809,331	2,774,988	29.2 %
Big Six	4	121,212	236,056	51.3 %
Baccarat	2	286,557	2,407,219	11.9 %
Minibaccarat	2	115,834	847,853	13.7 %
Other (Red Dog & Sic Bo)	3	54,473	211,439	25.8 %
Total - Table Games	**100**	**6,990,004**	**43,281,574**	**16.2 %**
			Handle	
Coin Oper Machines				
$ .05 Slot Machines	102	214,762	1,572,560	13.7 %
$ .25 Slot Machines	593	3,251,091	25,865,598	12.6 %
$1.00 Slot Machines	193	1,722,776	18,882,083	9.1 %
Other Slot Machines	798	5,131,360	59,112,855	8.7 %
Total - Coin Oper. Machines	**1686**	**10,319,898**	**105,433,096**	**9.8 %**
Total Casino Revenues		**$ 17,309,993**		

Sands Hotel and Casino
for the month of January, 1992

Casino Revenues	Authorized Units	Win	Drop	Win Percentage
Table Game				
Blackjack	59	3,192,560	23,262,063	13.7 %
Craps	17	2,500,695	14,342,294	17.4 %
Roulette	13	839,632	3,905,052	21.5 %
Big Six	3	106,899	222,800	48.0 %
Baccarat	4	951,630	6,586,950	14.4 %
Minibaccarat	2	154,829	1,091,476	14.2 %
Other (Red Dog & Sic Bo)	2	67,496	169,892	39.7 %
Total - Table Games	100	7,813,741	49,580,527	15.8 %
			Handle	
Coin Oper Machines				
$ .05 Slot Machines	71	212,496	1,310,111	16.2 %
$ .25 Slot Machines	418	2,477,037	16,929,177	14.6 %
$1.00 Slot Machines	194	1,504,799	15,096,422	10.0 %
Other Slot Machines	713	5,388,512	58,184,036	9.3 %
Total - Coin Oper. Machines	1396	9,582,844	91,519,746	10.5 %
Total Casino Revenues		$ 17,396,585		

Showboat
for the month of January, 1992

Casino Revenues	Authorized Units	Win	Drop	Win Percentage
Table Game				
Blackjack	46	2,580,535	16,136,825	16.0 %
Craps	16	2,081,891	12,540,211	16.6 %
Roulette	10	522,119	2,230,480	23.4 %
Big Six	1	67,941	177,386	38.3 %
Baccarat	3	551,937	2,836,574	19.5 %
Minibaccarat	2	57,772	464,905	12.4 %
Other (Red Dog & Sic Bo)	2	46,816	187,583	25.0 %
Total - Table Games	80	5,909,011	34,573,964	17.1 %
			Handle	
Coin Oper Machines				
$ .05 Slot Machines	96	353,602	2,502,565	14.1 %
$ .25 Slot Machines	663	4,786,373	40,648,473	11.8 %
$1.00 Slot Machines	194	1,932,459	22,151,173	8.7 %
Other Slot Machines	943	6,714,807	80,045,873	8.4 %
Total - Coin Oper. Machines	1896	13,787,241	145,348,084	9.5 %
Total Casino Revenues		$ 19,696,252		

Tropworld Casino and Entertainment Resort
for the month of January, 1992

Casino Revenues	Authorized Units	Win	Drop	Win Percentage
Table Game				
Blackjack	97	3,005,213	21,399,113	14.0 %
Craps	20	1,810,438	12,039,366	15.0 %
Roulette	16	853,289	3,453,991	24.7 %
Big Six	3	100,830	170,243	59.2 %
Baccarat	3	310,364	2,729,222	11.4 %
Minibaccarat	2	305,257	1,675,723	18.2 %
Other (Red Dog & Sic Bo)	5	115,337	328,545	35.1 %
Total - Table Games	**146**	**6,500,728**	**41,796,203**	**15.6 %**
			Handle	
Coin Oper Machines				
$ .05 Slot Machines	122	166,545	989,919	16.8 %
$ .25 Slot Machines	492	2,778,336	23,031,000	12.1 %
$1.00 Slot Machines	227	2,585,085	29,136,266	8.9 %
Other Slot Machines	1,586	9,965,412	123,876,038	8.0 %
Total - Coin Oper. Machines	**2,427**	**15,495,378**	**177,033,223**	**8.8 %**
Total Casino Revenues		**$ 21,996,106**		

Trump Castle Hotel and Casino
for the month of January, 1992

Casino Revenues	Authorized Units	Win	Drop	Win Percentage
Table Game				
Blackjack	56	2,869,268	18,685,161	15.4 %
Craps	17	2,246,348	14,145,368	15.9 %
Roulette	12	757,510	2,571,470	27.5 %
Big Six	2	64,319	151,844	42.4 %
Baccarat	3	228,398	2,393,099	9.5 %
Minibaccarat	2	129,661	1,090,959	11.9 %
Other (Red Dog & Sic Bo)	3	182,685	371,610	49.2 %
Total - Table Games	**95**	**6,478,189**	**39,589,511**	**16.4 %**
			Handle	
Coin Oper Machines				
$ .05 Slot Machines	49	191,779	1,423,109	13.5 %
$ .25 Slot Machines	547	3,505,002	30,067,491	11.7 %
$1.00 Slot Machines	213	1,675,456	17,864,720	9.4 %
Other Slot Machines	784	5,956,258	68,942,411	8.6 %
Total - Coin Oper. Machines	**1,593**	**11,328,495**	**18,297,731**	**9.6 %**
Total Casino Revenues		**$ 17,806,684**		

Trump Plaza
for the month of January, 1992

Casino Revenues	Authorized Units	Win	Drop	Win Percentage
Table Game				
Blackjack	67	3,195,069	24,757,079	12.9 %
Craps	16	1,986,084	12,968,401	15.3 %
Roulette	13	1,202,466	4,554,876	26.4 %
Big Six	3	157,812	337,194	46.8 %
Baccarat	2	3,959,752	9,701,873	40.8 %
Minibaccarat	3	433,985	2,092,703	20.7 %
Other (Red Dog & Sic Bo)	2	113,585	384,295	29.6 %
Total - Table Games	**106**	**11,048,753**	**54,796,421**	**20.2 %**
Coin Oper Machines			Handle	
$ .05 Slot Machines	84	297,050	1,816,907	16.3 %
$ .25 Slot Machines	539	2,987,092	22,593,119	13.2 %
$1.00 Slot Machines	203	1,972,946	23,031,398	8.6 %
Other Slot Machines	847	5,601,907	64,273,619	8.7 %
Total - Coin Oper. Machines	**1,673**	**10,858,995**	**111,715,043**	**9.7 %**
Total Casino Revenues		**$ 21,907,748**		

Trump Taj Mahal Casino Resort
for the month of January, 1992

Casino Revenues	Authorized Units	Win	Drop	Win Percentage
Table Game				
Blackjack	99	6,268,841	39,214,052	16.0 %
Craps	30	3,524,114	21,676,496	16.3 %
Roulette	21	1,572,530	5,930,925	26.5 %
Big Six	6	237,617	475,051	50.0 %
Baccarat	4	973,237	10,495,385	9.3 %
Minibaccarat	2	514,312	2,760,984	18.6 %
Other (Red Dog & Sic Bo)	3	164,318	472,302	34.8 %
Total - Table Games	**165**	**13,254,969**	**81,025,195**	**16.4 %**
			Handle	
Coin Oper Machines				
$ .05 Slot Machines	157	508,778	3,339,703	15.2 %
$ .25 Slot Machines	1,218	5,909,153	48,644,260	12.1 %
$1.00 Slot Machines	270	2,172,595	24,476,448	8.9 %
Other Slot Machines	1,089	7,547,278	83,849,353	9.0 %
Total - Coin Oper. Machines	**2,734**	**16,137,804**	**160,309,764**	**10.1 %**
Total Casino Revenues		**$ 29,392,773**		

**Look for these other exciting new books
by Zeke Feinberg
in your bookstore soon**

CASINO CRAPS - EARN $12 TO $24 PER HOUR
PLAYING CASINO CRAPS - "BEAT the
RECESSION"

CASINO CRAPS CHATTER

CASINO CRAPS FOR HIGH ROLLERS
HARD COVER - LIMITED EDITION

CASINO CRAPS - PLACE BETS & VIGORISH

CASINO CRAPS - HORNS, WHIRLS, HI-LO-YO
CRAPS & HARDWAYS

CASINO CRAPS - WOEFUL PASS LINE BETTOR
and the PARADOX of the WRONG
BETTOR

CASINO CRAPS - For NOVICE PLAYERS
Casino Craps is NOT for GAMBLING
Casino Craps is for EXCITING
ENTERTAINMENT

CASINO CRAPS - PROBABILITIES & ODDS

CASINO CRAPS - LIVE CASINO ACTION
FINANCIAL RESULTS USING MANY
DIFFERENT METHODS

SIC BO

On the
Social and
Emotional
Lives of
Gifted
Children

Tracy L. Cross, Ph.D.

PRUFROCK PRESS, INC.

Graphic and Cover Design by James Kendrick
Cover Artwork © EyeWire, Inc.

Printed in the United States of America.

ISBN 1-882664-73-6

Prufrock Press, Inc.
P.O. Box 8813
Waco, Texas 76714-8813
(800) 998-2208
Fax (800) 240-0333
http://www.prufrock.com

I dedicate this book
to the memory of Ronald R. Allen
and
to my favorite unsung heroes,
Eva Ruth Cross
and
Jennifer Cross.

Table of Contents

Preface

I have always been a psychologist and aspiring philosopher. As a young child, I often pondered the nature of people, why some had to starve while others wasted resources, why some made friends so easily and others seemed to be left out. I wondered how it was possible that some incredibly nice, warm, and caring people could also be racists. I remember concluding at age 6 that everything existed in abundance, just the ratios and proportions seemed out of balance. This was one of my earliest theories. I called it the "cattywompus world." Psyche had me from an early age. These same issues in one form or another still dominate my thinking today.

My best friend from age 3, Rick Allen, had an older brother named Ron whom I could tell did not quite fit in with any group of people. While my friends occasionally made fun of him for being "different," the adults seemed to be both intrigued and entertained by him. I often watched him out of the corner of my eye, fascinated by this extraordinary young mind. He truly aspired to be president, but first he needed to go to Yale. Tall order for a 6-year-old. While my friends and I practiced football, Ron was creating plans for his ascent to the Presidency. Ron did graduate from Yale University Law

School, and he did become president, not of the United States, but of the International Young Trial Lawyers Association. Ron died in an unfortunate swimming accident at age 44. He lived a productive and meaningful life working on behalf of others. This book is in the memory of Ron and the Allen family, one of the earliest and most important influences in my choosing this career path.

Other key events drew me into the field of gifted studies. Some are obvious to catalog while others remain unknown to me. An important awareness I came to as a teenager was how bright my mother was. I also came to understand how her circumstances, having grown up on a farm and graduating from a small, rural high school as valedictorian at age 15, led her down a path of unfulfilled promise. An early marriage, four children in six years, and the typical sacrifices made by her generation of adults destined her to live her short 48 years as an unsung hero. The times and circumstances in which my mother grew up clearly delimited her opportunities in life. This book is also dedicated to her memory.

As a teenager I had the fortune of working at my family's art gallery. I studied the artists who spent untold hours at the gallery interacting with Knoxville's "old money" and "nouveau riche." I learned from this experience that some extraordinarily talented people struggle to live by certain societal rules. I watched as several of these artists/professors at the local university self-destructed. I learned that society's expectations can be brutal reminders of the consequences of being gifted. I also learned that there can be brutal consequences to being gifted, due simply to society's expectations.

My wife and I met while in high school. I became close to her gifted siblings; five children identified as academically gifted in one family. I studied them for years as I became a young man. In addition, I was quite aware during my teenage years of the surreal quality of high schools. I found the academic experience of being a student in my high school much like being a subject in the control group of an experiment: lit-

tle desirable impact, but still subject to all that exists in the social hierarchy of a school setting. I also learned that playing sports had the power of making one popular even against his or her will. At the same time, being introverted was unacceptable to most, teachers and students alike.

In graduate school, I met Larry Coleman. We worked together evaluating the Tennessee Governor's School and studied the experience of gifted students. Over the past 17 years, Larry and I have focused on the lives of gifted students in various types of settings and locations. We have produced numerous articles, chapters, and one textbook entitled *Being Gifted in School: An Introduction to Development, Guidance, and Teaching*. Larry's guidance and inspiration have been invaluable to me in my professional development.

This book was inspired by all these important people who taught me many life lessons. The actual idea for creating this book, however, came from Sally Reis, who encouraged me to compile these columns into a book. I am thankful to Sally for her kind words that led me to pursue this endeavor.

The text for this book was written over the past seven years. The material, with one exception, is made up of the regular columns I wrote for *Gifted Child Today*. The exception is an invited piece for the December 1999 issue of *GCT* wherein a number of professionals in the field were asked to contribute our top 10 list of important events influencing the field of gifted education over the past century.

Originally, the columns were going to be included in the order of their appearance in the journal with only very minor editing. During the editing process, my wife noticed that there was a natural pattern that might help those reading this book to better follow the material. Consequently, the columns have been organized into four themes: About Gifted Children: Who They Are and Why; Guiding Gifted Children; Gifted Children Today; and Where We Have Been and Where We are Going. I hope that the chapters contained in each of these thematic sections provide ideas helpful in understanding the

social and emotional development of gifted students and how teachers, counselors, and parents can work together to guide their development.

Several people worked very hard to complete this book. I would like to thank Jennifer Cross for helping me throughout the project by editing, proofreading, and suggesting the final organization. She also helped me during the original writing phase of the columns that appeared in *GCT*. I would like to thank Jim and Christy Kendrick for carrying out all the necessary editorial work to bring this project to fruition. I also want to thank Joel McIntosh for supporting many of my efforts over the past nine years. And, a final note of thanks go to my children, Ian, Keenan, Colin, and Eva, for reminding me on a daily basis of the importance of advocating for gifted students.

Introduction: A Continuum of Psychological Services

To understand the social and emotional development of gifted students, one must consider many issues and concerns. For example, those who have written on the subject over the past quarter-century or so have tended to speak to the following issues: gifted students have social and emotional needs, gifted students' needs are often unique to them, there are specific characteristics of gifted students, and the characteristics create or reflect needs. A much smaller group of authors has written that gifted students tend to experience life in much the same way as their nongifted peers, that their social and emotional needs are often determined by the qualities of the environment in which they find themselves, and that there are few, if any, characteristics that are the same across gifted students. Some areas of agreement have been that gifted children are, in fact, children first, that early experiences in life are important as they develop, and that adults have important roles to play in the social and emotional development of gifted students.

To help provide a framework for understanding the ideas in this book, I have created a Continuum of Psychological Services that illustrates the wide range of needs gifted students have and the potential role that differing groups of adults need to help

them play. The Continuum of Psychological Services also makes it evident that parents, teachers, and counselors need to work together to cover most of the services the gifted students will need and that no one person can play all the roles needed.

Continuum of Psychological Services

Advising	Guidance	Counseling	Therapy	Psychopharmacology
parents	parents	counselors	psychologists	psychiatrists
teachers	teachers	psychologists	psychiatrists	physicians
counselors	counselors			
friends	friends			
siblings	siblings			

In this Continuum of Psychological Services, advising is the broadest need area. This includes general life advice, such as how to choose a tie, or more specific information, such as what courses to consider taking. Because of the broad range of activities and the level of expertise needed, more individuals will be capable of providing this service to gifted children.

The guidance position is slightly more focused than advising in that it tends to deal mostly with academic or school-related matters. These can vary significantly from course selection to relationship building. Teachers are often key to providing guidance to students on a daily basis. Guidance counselors provide this service to a few students and generally with a higher level of professional preparation.

The counseling position requires more specific training in counseling theories and techniques than the previous two positions. This category overlaps with both advising and therapy. I see it as different in that it naturally tends to revolve around school-based matters, and there is always a large, built-in clientele for a school counselor.

The fourth position of therapy is broader than counseling in the sense that it can pertain to almost any presenting problem. It is different than counseling in that therapy can take years to complete, is typically done outside schools, and often involves seeing a therapist in a private setting. Therapy often deals with much more serious or dangerous problems than does school counseling.

The final position on the continuum is that of psychopharmacology. I use this term because of the current pattern in our culture of parents seeking medical treatments for behavioral problems. This pattern often yields some form of drug therapy. Psychiatrists and family physicians are typically the professionals who deliver this type of service.

While I recognize that my Continuum of Psychological Services is rather elementary, and clearly one could argue for different interpretations of the roles of each group and the overlap across services, the value of the Continuum is that it illustrates the need for collaboration across groups of people. For example, if a parent has a concern about a child, quite possibly the child's teacher and others have some important information to share. Without efforts of collaboration, the parent can only hold one perspective of the child. This need for collaboration guarantees that multiple perspectives in differing settings can be included in a discussion. The Continuum also establishes a pattern for who to pursue first based on the kind of issue or concern that exists.

The remainder of the book is a reflection of my thinking about the lives of gifted students. I have tried to report on research and be clear when I am offering my own opinion. In either case, these writings reflect personal and professional biases of which the reader should be aware. The first is the eclectic nature I bring to the study of this phenomenon. To that end, I use psychological, educational, sociological, and anthropological data.

A second bias I have is that I believe all people live in differing subcultures that are very much impacted by their time

in history. Consequently, the study of gifted students necessarily must take these factors into consideration.

A third bias is that I believe people are influenced by their own sense of human agency. And, while genetic predispositions clearly exist and are important, I believe that the developing person is able to change over time in ways reflecting the interaction with their environment.

Another bias that influences my thinking is that I believe theories are just that—theories—educated social constructions subject to evolution over time with additional information and in differing contexts. I believe that the construct of giftedness necessarily must be considered in light of societal values and with an awareness of dominant subgroups. In an effort to transcend all these biases, I try to seek many forms of data, including those that do not maintain the highest level of status in our current social structure. I see skepticism as an important part of the interpretation of any theory or "statement of fact." I encourage all readers to develop a healthy sense of skepticism—not cynicism, rather, your ability to question what others may accept as fact. This book represents my perspective on the social and emotional needs of gifted children, colored by my experience and beliefs. Your perspective should inform your interpretation of my works, as well as the works of others.

About Gifted Children: Who They Are and Why

This section contains five columns, all of which focus on a description of the gifted child. In my first column for *GCT*, "Examining Beliefs about the Gifted," I felt it was important to present some information about myself and how I have come to believe what I have about gifted children. The primary thrust of this column is that I do believe that there is such an entity as a gifted child and that we should be cautious not to impose one dominant perspective on our efforts to identify the social and emotional needs of this widely diverse group.

In "Determining the Needs of Gifted Children," I discuss the difficulty in determining the social and emotional needs or "issues" that are unique to gifted children. This is not an easy

task because so much of what we believe on the matter has been determined before the completion of substantial research.

My research into the suicides of three students associated with a residential high school for gifted students led me to publish two columns on this very important and serious topic. The first of these two columns is placed in this section because of its emphasis on gifted adolescents who have committed suicide and how difficult it is to know more about these troubled children. The column also attempts to provide guidance to adults about what can and should be done to avoid suicidal behavior of gifted students.

For years, while interacting with gifted children, their parents, and teachers, ideas about who gifted children are and what makes them different from others troubled me. I was finally able to draw many of these ideas together in my column titled "A Consideration of Axiomatic Statements." These statements offer in a nutshell many of the principles that underly my beliefs about guiding gifted children. It is important for those who work with gifted children to remember that they are children and people just like everyone else. The exceptionalities we see are not the *only* aspect to a gifted child's development and may not even be the most significant one. These axiomatic statements provide a strong foundation for an understanding of the mixed messages gifted students receive on a daily basis. "How Gifted Students Cope With Mixed Messages" takes a look at some of the research Larry Coleman and I have done into how students deal with the expectations society places on gifted students.

This group of columns sets the stage for an understanding of who gifted students are, and I hope they will give you pause as you examine your beliefs about them.

On the Social and Emotional Lives of Gifted Children

Examining Beliefs About the Gifted

hen I first began writing a regular column for *Gifted Child Today* addressing salient issues pertaining to social and emotional needs of gifted students, I felt it most appropriate to outline how I hoped to develop the column over time. My first step was to introduce myself in an effort to provide the readership enough information to make an informed decision about whether or not to read the column. This is important information for readers of this book, as well.

I hold a doctoral degree in educational psychology from the University of Tennessee—Knoxville. My original training was very quantitative in nature. Later, however, I took additional coursework and also apprenticed for three years under the tutelage of a phenomenologist. I have been a college professor at a land-grant university, two state universities, and a small liberal arts college and have studied gifted students throughout the nation. For the past four years, I have served as the executive director for a state-funded resi-

dential school for academically gifted adolescents. Even though I realize that this information is far more interesting to me than it is to you, I am quite sure that each of these facts has influenced my views of the world. So, *caveat emptor*!

In the *GCT* columns and in this book, I tried to provide information and ideas that would pique the interest of some, prompt hallway conversations among some, and, perhaps, raise the dander of others. To that end, my approach varies from offering basic factual information to arguing points through syllogism, to reporting on studies I have conducted. I try to present at least two major lines of thought on important topics and often try to situate the focus of each chapter within the research base, while at the same time elucidating concerns about how we have come to hold certain beliefs. To reach these goals, I tried to write the columns that have been adapted into this book in a style that would be as accessible to as large an audience as possible.

Clarifying Beliefs About the Gifted

The topic of discussion, the social and emotional needs of gifted students, presupposes some important beliefs. Some of those include that gifted people do exist; they are identifiable, we have established a process to identify them, and, consequently, we have identified them (at least enough of them to educate our biases); those we have identified represent the real thing; and once we have identified them, we can make reasonable decisions about what their social and emotional needs are.

Unless I am wrong about this rather elementary syllogism, any broken link might cast doubt on the general topic of debate, or at least limit what is knowable about the topic. In this first column, I will discuss a few of these assumptions.

Is there evidence that gifted people do exist? At this point, I feel quite comfortable in claiming that most educators would acknowledge that some people manifest extraordinary abilities. We have heard of or personally know people who seem to

read markedly better, run faster, jump higher, do high-level mathematics before they can talk, paint remarkable works of art, or play the piano masterfully at an early age. In short, human variation stares us in the face every day of our lives. Hence, gifted people do seem to exist.

There are at least two approaches we use to come to grips with the manifest differences across people. The first is to conclude that people who do not demonstrate the exceptional qualities previously listed are less than adequate, while the second approach is to label the aforementioned people as exceptional and call them *gifted*. I like the second option better myself. As reasonable as this logic may seem on the surface, the decision to establish nongifted folks as normal has some important intellectual baggage. For example, when I think of the term *needs* (as in social and emotional needs of the gifted), I reflect upon my upbringing when my parents would attempt to teach me a lesson. The lesson usually began with a statement like "Tracy, you need to . . . " I remember thinking, "According to you, I may need to, but to me I am okay with the way I am currently doing it."

In short, by establishing the gifted as different, we become normal, thus elevating ourselves into the position of deciding what the needs of gifted people are.

The term *needs* is considered by some as a direct reflection of the values of a dominant group in society. Moreover, much of the research conducted on this topic has been done over the past 60 years. During this time, many groups of people (e.g., Native Americans, African Americans, Hispanic Americans) have been conspicuously missing from the ranks of the identified gifted. Therefore, we should be aware of the historical context and the absence of voice reflected in many of the studies seeking to shed light on the needs of gifted children.

Defining Terms

A final point is that one of the difficult aspects of being considerate when trying to understand the needs of gifted stu-

dents is that social and emotional needs may not be static. That is to say, the environment in which one exists may greatly impact these needs, or the mere definition of need has to be contextualized.

In short, at this point in history we can say that serious consideration must be given to the terminology used to describe gifted students and its relationship to cultural power, the voices that are missing from the dialogue, and the relative influence or determination of environmental factors on the nature of the needs of the gifted. Food for thought.

So, as we continue this dialogue, I assert that it would be prudent to constantly remind ourselves to question from whose perspective we are establishing and defining the nature of the social and emotional needs of gifted students.

Determing
the Needs
of Gifted Children

T his chapter will pick up where the first one left off by posing two questions frequently asked about gifted students: Do gifted students really have social and emotional needs and, if they have these needs, are they the same as their nongifted peers?

For years, researchers, clinicians, and educators have tried to untangle the complicated relationships among the general ability, family dynamics, specific culture, and school experiences of children in order to build models of the social and emotional development of gifted children. From the myriad studies cutting across the psychological paradigms and the concomitant research techniques employed, I feel it has been established that children do develop emotionally and socially and, consequently, do have needs or, perhaps more appropriately stated, issues in these areas. An important contribution to the research base was by Thomas Buescher (1985) in an article entitled "A Framework for Understanding the Social and Emotional Development of Gifted and Talented Students." In this article, he outlined a

developmental framework to be used for identifying social and emotional concerns of gifted students. The framework includes six "Dynamic Issues of Giftedness During Adolescence":

Ownership: Who says I am gifted anyhow?
Dissonance: Recurrent tension between my performance and my own expectations.
Risk-Taking: Should I be taking new risks or seeking secure situations?
Others'
Expectations: Being pushed by others' expectations, being pulled by my own needs.
Impatience: I have to know the answer right now!
Identity: What counts is who I am. (p. 14)

This framework allows us to identify possible needs of gifted children based upon the qualities and issues relevant to the individual child, rather than trying to create an omnibus list of needs for all gifted children. This is an important point and will be discussed as part of the response to the second question.

Now, on to the question about whether the social and emotional needs of gifted children are different from those of their nongifted peers. There are two lines of thought on this question. The traditional consideration is that differences need to be ferreted out if they exist, which suggests the importance of distinctions being made across needs between gifted and nongifted children. The alternative consideration is that it really matters not whether the differences exist as long as the phenomenon of what gifted children's social and emotional needs are has been captured and depicted. In short, focus on what is for gifted children without regard for their nongifted peers. One of the reasons this debate is important is that the two research positions often lead to differing research approaches being taken. In turn, the approaches define what

is knowable about the social and emotional needs of gifted children. And, like viewing the world through an eye patch on either the right or left eye, one's perception of reality is always attenuated by the view.

I believe that there is not sufficient evidence in the research lore to unequivocally claim that gifted children have social and emotional needs that are qualitatively different from or mutually exclusive of their nongifted peers. Having said this, I will discuss two issues that I think are critical to my position. The first was noted previously: the search for omnibus needs that cut across all gifted children is misguided. The second is that the differences in needs are likely a function of the relationship of the individual child's talents and his or her social interactions within the prominent communities of his or her world (e.g. family and school).

In the politics of research exploration, there is a desire to build a model or list of needs that encompasses all children. This goal fuels and is fueled by the common wisdom, myths, and speculation about what gifted children's needs might be. In my opinion, not enough consideration has been given to other qualities and experiences the gifted child has that would influence his or her needs. For example, lists abound of the nature and needs and the characteristics of gifted children. These lists include claims that are always wide ranging and often inconsistent. And, at the same time, we have all known students who fit some or much of the information not on the list. To rectify this situation, I recommend we redefine the concern from that of need by using the term Buescher and others have used: *issue*. The question would change to "What are the social and emotional issues of gifted children?"

As the research base on the social and emotional development of gifted children grows, along with the evolving research approaches being taken, a clear message is emerging. That is, the culture in which a child is immersed has an important influence on the experience of being gifted. The cultural values interact with the social goals of the student and

the issues associated with growing up in America. Therefore, the social and emotional needs of any particular gifted child may be predictable, but cannot be decided a priori. In short, although the characteristics of the gifted child, along with certain environmental factors, might create conditions where needs should exist, unless the individual child perceives or experiences the needs, they do not exist—no matter what a list might include or expert might say.

So what can we say? Where can we turn for reasonable information? I suggest that, if you are interested in reviewing some of the salient research on the topic that reflects these two lines of thought, you should consider the following authors. Dr. Linda K. Silverman is a leader in the field who has written a textbook on counseling the gifted in which she discusses her beliefs about what the social and emotional needs are and how to address them from a clinician's perspective. Laurence J. Coleman represents an alternative line of thinking that can be reviewed in his 1985 textbook, *Schooling the Gifted* (Addison-Wesley), and in miscellaneous articles (e.g., "Is Being Gifted a Social Handicap?" [1988], which I co-authored). Coleman emphasizes the influence the relationship between the environment of a school and the gifted child's desire to feel accepted in the environment has on his or her social and emotional needs. Both Silverman and Coleman are fine researchers who provide worthwhile perspectives on the social and emotional needs of gifted children.

Examining Claims About Gifted Children and Suicide

This chapter deals with a very sobering topic, one that appears too often in the newspapers, elicits strong opinions, and strikes fear in the hearts of parents: the suicides of gifted adolescents. In the following pages, I will provide an overview of what can and cannot be said on the topic based on actual research. I will focus my comments on gifted adolescents, even though preadolescents have died by their own hand. I will limit my comments to adolescents since they constitute by far the greater percentage of suicides (as compared to pre-teens) and since there is more *information* available on this age group. Please note the term *information* rather than data. This distinction foreshadows the paucity of research on the topic that will be discussed.

One characteristic of our culture is the growing rate of its population that commits suicide. Increases over the past decade are seen in virtually every age group, with the 15–24 age range showing significant increases. Suicide ranks as the second leading cause of death among young people (Capuzzi

& Golden, 1988). One should note that adults older than 70 years have shown large increases in their suicide rate over the past 20 years. Within the large group of school-age children are subgroups that have a much higher rate of suicide than the rate for the entire group. For example, troubled adolescents have been estimated to attempt suicide at a rate of 33% (Tomlinson-Keasey & Keasey, 1988). From these studies, we can conclude that the rate of adolescent suicide has risen over the past decade, as have the rates of other groups. We can also conclude that subgroups vary in their rate of suicide.

A significant contribution of previous research on adolescent suicide has been the determination that there are significant risk factors:

- psychiatric disorders, such as depression and anxiety;
- drug and alcohol abuse;
- genetic factors;
- family loss or disruption;
- friend or family member of suicide victim;
- homosexuality;
- rapid socio-cultural change;
- media emphasis on suicide;
- impulsiveness and aggressiveness; and
- ready access to lethal methods (Davidson & Linnoila, 1991).

One question I am often asked is whether the suicide rates of gifted adolescents differ significantly from the larger population of adolescents. In my own research, colleagues and I have conducted psychological autopsies of three gifted adolescents who committed suicide. In our literature review, we found several interesting patterns.

. The first pattern was the tendency for authors to make conclusions and recommendations about the incidence and nature of gifted suicide without supporting data. Moreover, general findings from marginally related studies were used to support

the contention that the rate of suicide among gifted adolescents is the same as or lower than the larger population of adolescents. Again, these statements were based on no direct evidence.

The second pattern was the tendency of authors to cite each others' work based upon speculation. The net effect was the reification of that speculation. This pattern exists throughout research bodies and is not unique to this lore. What makes this research body different is that there is virtually no true research at the foundation of the base, yet truisms abound.

A third and more subtle pattern in the lore was the tendency for authors to advocate for gifted children amidst their manuscripts. Some of the pieces seemed less like efforts at research and more like efforts at protecting the image of gifted children.

Gifted Suicide Rates

Let me reiterate what was most often suggested in the literature: that the suicide rate of gifted adolescents is the same as or lower than the general population of adolescents. The basis for this claim is conceptual, not empirical. In fact, there is so little evidence available about gifted adolescents on this specific topic that nothing should be concluded. In other words, at this point, we cannot know.

Although seemingly an innocuous difference in assessments, the ramifications can vary significantly. For example, there is a growing number of academics considering the population of gifted adolescents in smaller, more representative subgroups than in an omnibus fashion. In this case, students with differing characteristics might have markedly different incidents of suicide during adolescence. Some evidence for this claim can be found in research that has studied the lives of a large group of eminent people in the artistic and literary world. Among this subgroup, Ludwig (1995) found a higher incidence of suicide by the age of 30. He also found that "investigative types" (e.g., scientists) committed suicide at a higher rate than the general population after the age of 60. I

must interject a serious note of caution here. These data were drawn from a much older population, and, given the nature of the risk factors often associated with suicide, there may be a limited ability to generalize the findings. So, even though it stands to reason that subgroups of adolescents are at greater risk of committing suicide than other groups, there is not enough evidence to conclude whether or not gifted adolescents per se have a higher-than-average-risk.

Some Reasons
There Are Few Studies to Draw On

There are several reasons why there have been few studies conducted on the suicides of gifted students. A few include:

- the current data collected nationally about adolescent suicide do not include whether or not the child was gifted;
- the varying definitions of gifted and talented used across the United States make it difficult to know whether a child who committed suicide was gifted;
- issues of confidentiality limit access to data;
- conducting psychological autopsies of suicide victims is an expensive endeavor in terms of time and money;
- the fact that more adolescents than preadolescents commit suicide combined with the fact that secondary schools are not as actively engaged in identifying gifted students makes conducting research on this topic more difficult; and
- the terminal nature of suicide requires certain types of information to be garnered after the event.

Promising Studies

I am aware of a handful of studies that show promise of contributing to the research lore in significant ways. Two are

looking specifically at suicide ideation, one at the secondary level and one among honors students in college. A third study showing promise is the psychological autopsies previously noted. Combined, they will add significantly to the current level of understanding.

One interesting question that recognizes human variation within the gifted population deals with a topic of considerable debate among academics. That is, "What specific role, if any, do the qualities that some gifted adolescents possess play in their suicides?" For example, possible connections between gifted children's unusual sensitivities and perfectionism (Delisle, 1986) and isolationism and introversion (Kaiser & Berndt, 1985) with suicidal behavior have been raised. In the psychological autopsies being conducted, we have found that Piechowski's treatment of Dabrowski's theories have been helpful in interpreting the data collected. Some of the characteristics we have found beneficial in the data analysis phase include: intellectual-introspection, avid reading, curiosity, imaginational-fantasy, animistic and magical thinking, mixing truth and fiction, illusions, being emotional, strong affective memory, concern with death, depressive and suicidal moods, sensitivity in relationships, and feelings of inadequacy and inferiority (Piechowski, 1979).

What can we say about the suicides of gifted adolescents?

- Adolescents are committing suicide.
- Gifted adolescents are committing suicide.
- The rate of suicide has increased over the past decade for the general population of adolescents within the context of an overall increase across all age groups.
- It is reasonable to conclude that the incidence of suicide of gifted adolescents has increased over the past decade while keeping in mind that there are no definitive data on the subject.

- Given the limited data available, we cannot ascertain whether the incidence of suicide among gifted adolescents is different from among the general population of adolescents.

A Consideration of Axiomatic Statements

n this chapter, I would like to remind teachers, parents, and counselors of some of the most important influences on the psychological development of gifted students. With an awareness of these influences, adults can more effectively guide and nurture the development of these children in the social and emotional realms.

I hope to clarify these concepts with axiomatic statements that illustrate many of the salient considerations across the life of a gifted student. Perhaps this will help you think of the ways in which gifted students are the same as others, different from others, and how they are impacted by outside influences.

- *Gifted students share many developmental characteristics and problems with all people.*

Gifted students are children first; as such, they have much in common with children of average ability.

People develop over time; as people, gifted students develop over time.

Because talents manifest in numerous domains, children remain a very heterogeneous group of people; as children, few to no claims would be equally true for the entire group of gifted students.

Every child grows up in a different environment; as children, gifted students grow up in different environments.

People are agents in their own lives; as people, gifted students are agents in their own lives.

Children vary in a multitude of personal characteristics; as children, gifted students vary in a multitude of personal characteristics.

People need to feel accepted; as people, gifted students need to feel accepted.

Knowledge is largely believed to be a construction of the person. As a subset of one's knowledge base, social cognition is developed idiosyncratically through the eyes of an immature mind.

Influencing the perceptions a person has about his or her life that were formed at an early age is often a difficult endeavor; as people, it is also difficult to influence the perceptions formed early in the lives of gifted students.

Influences on the belief systems and behaviors of children begin with parents, continue with family members, but often are transcended by peer influence as the children get older, with the potential of significant others influencing them as they mature; as children, the same pattern is true for gifted students.

A person's development is idiosyncratic; hence, patterns of development for gifted students will probably not closely reflect developmental milestones that are derived by averaging across groups of people.

Environmental influences on a child can never transcend biologically based potential; as children, this is true for gifted students, as well.

- *Gifted students have life experiences and issues that are different just because they are gifted.*

Because they have extraordinary capabilities, gifted students will likely experience certain aspects of the world differently from those who do not share the same gifts or talents.

Giftedness is often experienced as feeling different from other students and, unlike other exceptionalities, can be hidden. Consequently, gifted students as agents in their own lives behave in compliance with their survival needs and social goals.

- *Influences outside the individual have an impact on gifted students.*

Groups of people in society are treated differently relative to opportunities, expectations, and stereotypes; as people, gifted students' experiences will be affected by variables they cannot control.

Definitions of giftedness change over time and vary in different societies. Whether or not children are thought to be gifted, how they are treated, and what subsequent perceptions and behaviors they engage in are variable and likely to be culturally relevant.

Americans maintain numerous views of gifted students simultaneously. Gifted students receive mixed messages about their places in society, and that is often interpreted to be an indicator of the degree to which they are accepted and can be themselves.

Schools tend to acknowledge and reward achievement over time (hence, labels such as *overachiever* are often given to gifted students to account for this prejudice for averaging achievement). Students of outstanding ability may be overlooked if their achievement is not consistently manifest (if gifted students manifest enough extraordinary work to be noticed, but not enough to satisfy others, they are labeled *underachiever*).

As gifted students get older, a primary task they have to complete in their psychological development is identity formation. Considering the axioms provided, one could argue that the various, simultaneous, and often contradictory messages gifted students receive during their lives, when screened through perceptions that were developed when they were very young, destine gifted students to engage in numerous patterns of social coping behavior. These observed patterns may appear unreasonable or naïve to adults who have not experienced the world in the manner in which gifted students do. The challenge that teachers, parents, and counselors of gifted students must meet is to create learning environments in which gifted students feel fully accepted and that are, at the same time, sophisticated in their approaches to developing the students' talents.

How Gifted Students Cope With Mixed Messages

I n the previous chapter entitled "A Consideration of Axiomatic Statements," I provided an overview of three categories of statements about the lives of gifted students. The first category was entitled "Gifted students share many developmental characteristics and problems with all people." It portrayed ways in which gifted children are like other children. The second category of axiomatic statements was called "Gifted students have life experiences and issues that are different just because they are gifted." This set of statements attempted to characterize some specific differences in experiences that gifted students have as compared to their nongifted peers. In the final set of statements, "Influences outside the individual have an impact on gifted students," I tried to illustrate how others' beliefs about giftedness potentially affect gifted students. The three sets of statements portrayed the lives of gifted students as existing within a world that sends them mixed messages that convey numerous unfavorable notions of the meaning of giftedness.

In this chapter, I am continuing the effort to illustrate how gifted students deal with these mixed messages. More specifically, I will relate what Larry Coleman and I have found to be a reasonable description of the experience of giftedness and how these students cope with life. From our research, we have posited that, for many gifted students, a figural aspect of the experience of giftedness is that of being stigmatized. Over the past 15 years, our research has shown time and again that this is an important component of the experience. In his book *Schooling the Gifted* (1985), Larry proposed a "Stigma of Giftedness Paradigm" that has three parts:

1. gifted students want to have normal social interactions;
2. they believe that others will treat them differently if they learn of their giftedness; and
3. gifted students learn that they can manage information about themselves in ways that enable them to maintain greater social latitude.

Patterns of Gifted Students' Coping Behaviors

Given this set of beliefs, gifted students become active agents in trying to establish for themselves, against the backdrop of mixed messages, a degree and type of social latitude and experience that minimizes pain while allowing them to deal with the issues that change as they develop. Many of their strategies are rather obvious, while others are tacit knowledge for them. The combined set of strategies was originally characterized on a Continuum of Visibility with Total Visibility (playing a stereotypic role associated with being gifted in order to stand out from others) on one end, Blending In (finding ways to avoid standing out from the larger group of students) in the middle, and Disidentifying (proactively engaging in behavior that one believes is associated with a subculture's stereotypes that is opposite the group of which the gifted child might naturally be a part) at the other end.

Continuum of Visibility

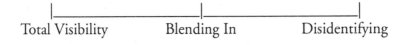

|_____|_____|
Total Visibility   Blending In   Disidentifying

For example, one student may choose to play the role of mad scientist to stand out as much as possible from others, while another chooses to navigate school along gender-typed expectations by sublimating academic interests with what they perceive as more acceptable behaviors, such as dating or competing in athletics. Other types of coping behaviors include underachieving in school and more serious efforts like suicide. Typically, however, the coping behaviors of gifted students tend to be less harmful, sometimes evolving into behaviors that have some benefit to their academic performance, such as studying more and reading to escape. Depending upon one's social goals, the behaviors of gifted students tend to fall into the categories listed on the continuum. With the exception of the Total Visibility category, the others reflect the students' desire to manage information. Consequently, their behaviors to that end are situation-specific; for example, not responding in school when a teacher asks a question (Blending In), or making friends with cliques of children in school whose reputation would be opposite that of gifted students (Disidentifying; e.g., becoming a "doper" instead of a "nerd").

My more recent research has caused me to add to the continuum a fourth position that reflects the most dire efforts at coping: taking one's own life. It fits the continuum notion in that the behaviors are coping efforts. It is different, however, in view of the fact that I am unsure of the extent to which the coping is more connected with managing giftedness and its interrelatedness with larger life issues, or merely an act most closely associated with depression and other correlates of suicide. We must concern ourselves, however, with the broader issue of the conditions in which gifted students live and what

we as adults (teachers, counselors, parents) do to assist their development and what we may unknowingly do to send them mixed messages. I believe that we need to take stock of our own beliefs about gifted students and seek additional training to prepare ourselves to assist in the development of all students.

The lives of gifted students are both the same as and quite different from other students' lives. Understanding the pain and suffering that children experience is only the beginning of what we as the nurturers of gifted students need to know. To minimize the mixed messages gifted students perceive, teachers, counselors, and parents must communicate expectations and beliefs held about giftedness. When they are congruent, the messages the students perceive will be more similar, thus allowing them to thrive. When the messages are dissimilar, gifted students will engage in numerous coping behaviors, many of which are detrimental to their development and success as students. If you would like to read in greater detail about the lives of gifted students from Larry's and my perspective, then I encourage you to read any of the references listed below.

Coleman, L. J. (1985). *Schooling the gifted.* New York: Addison Wesley.

Coleman, L. J., & Cross, T. L. (1988). Is being gifted a social handicap? *Journal for the Education of the Gifted, 11*, 41–56.

Cross, T. L., Coleman, L. J., & Terhaar-Yonkers. (1991). The social cognition of gifted adolescents in schools: Managing the stigma of giftedness. *Journal for the Education of the Gifted, 15*, 44–55.

Guiding
Gifted Children

O nce we know a little more about who gifted children are, it is important for us to use that knowledge to help them function successfully in their environment. Most of the chapters in this section appeared in order in *GCT* as a series of columns focusing on what I believe is important in this guidance process. The first three chapters in this section, "Guiding and Supporting the Development of Gifted Children," "Practical Advice for Guiding the Gifted," and "Working on Behalf of Gifted Students," offer ideas about things teachers, parents, and counselors should consider in their role and some specific things they can do for their young charges. I allude to the important role of communication in many of the suggestions

listed in these first three chapters; and, in the fourth, "Developing Relationships, Communication, and Identity," I focus on what can be a difficult aspect of childhood. Communicating with the adults in their lives, building relationships with other children, and developing their own sense of identity are all aspects of childhood that can be either traumatic or relatively easy. This chapter gives some suggestions for smoothing the path for gifted children.

The final chapter in this section was created from my research into gifted adolescent suicide. This chapter is a synopsis of the findings of a study my colleagues, Dr. Robert Cook and Dr. David Dixon, and I conducted on the lives of three adolescents who committed suicide. The detailed description of these adolescents and their circumstances were developed through a psychological autopsy process. Learning about these students led us to the development of specific recommendations for preventing suicides of gifted adolescents. I cannot emphasize enough the need to be on the lookout for indicators of suicidal behavior and the need to be proactive, no matter how uncomfortable you may feel in taking action. Professional counselors are key in the solution to the destructive notions these adolescents hold, but they can do nothing if adults are not aware of the need for their intervention.

Guiding
and Supporting
the Development
of Gifted Children

H aving spent several years conducting research, working directly with gifted students in the role of teacher, counselor, and program director, and reading others' studies on the topic of the social and emotional needs of gifted students, I have come to believe that there are several strategies that will help parents, teachers, and counselors guide gifted children.

Some of the topics have a substantial research base, some have only a modest research base, and some have little to no published research base supporting them. Cutting across these ideas is a form of conventional wisdom that I have seen expressed by many in the field. I suspect the reason that such widespread conventional wisdom exists is primarily due to the fact that our professional experiences become our primary source of data as we try to make sense of the world. Although I believe there is danger in relying too much on personal experiences when making generalizations, I do respect the fact that drawing on multiple forms of data, including personal experience, is an appropriate

method for making informed decisions. So, to break with my past practice of trying to forward only those ideas that have emerged from published research findings, I am going to provide a partial list of ideas that I believe have merit when trying to guide gifted children.

I will let my qualifiers reflect the degree of confidence that I have in these ideas. Some are speculative, while others are soundly supported by a research base. Some are taken from research in gifted education, some from outside the field, and some come largely from my own professional experience. Consider these ideas for teachers, counselors, and parents who guide the social and emotional development of gifted children:

1. As you consider your role in the development of a gifted child, realize that your best efforts cannot prevent all the struggles and emotional turmoil from occurring in the child's life. Your efforts may, however, allow the child to effectively transcend the difficulties associated with youth, and particularly those issues unique to gifted children.

2. Remember that the gifted child is a child first. Adults often forget that the young person with whom they are dealing is, in fact, a child. When listening to gifted children talk about academic topics, it is difficult to remember that they are very likely at the same general developmental level in the social and emotional domain as their nongifted peers. Treat children as young people first, and deal with their specific gifts second.

3. Communication among the three groups of adults (parents, teachers, counselors) is vital. Each group needs a clear understanding of the child and the parents' and teacher's goals for the child. These three groups of adults often have different goals for the students. Consequently, it is important to share appropriate information.

4. Try to understand the social milieu of the school or classroom through the eyes of the child. This is a difficult, but worthwhile task. I have been astounded and dismayed by

the extent to which the social expectations for students are never openly discussed or understood. Often, the teacher and other school personnel have quite divergent views of what it means to be a student or a gifted student. Moreover, students also hold a wide variety of opinions about what they think being a student means and how they should behave in various school settings. Therefore, talking openly about the expectations for students can help them feel more comfortable in the school.

5. Serve as a clearinghouse for information about gifted students. Share the information via meetings and by sharing literature. Since none of the three groups of adults (parents, teachers, counselors) receives significant training on the nature and needs of gifted students, it is important to create opportunities for them to learn how to be proactive in the child's life. The ERIC Clearinghouse has invaluable information prepared for this purpose. Other sources of information include local colleges and universities, state agencies, the National Association for Gifted Children, the Association for the Gifted, and the Internet.

6. Make available individual, group, and family counseling for gifted students and their families. Although relatively easy to organize, it is rarely done. If this is difficult to arrange, then share materials with each group (parents, teachers, counselors) as a means to better prepare the various professionals who work with gifted children.

7. Learn about the child's personality and social goals. This will enable all three groups to guide the child through the school years. When pursuing this strategy, be sure to include information from the field of "general" psychology. The vast majority of facts within the field of psychology are applicable to the lives of gifted students.

8. Teach the child to better understand his or her nature and anticipate how to react to events and circumstances in his or her life. Part of this understanding may be accomplished through personality and interest inventories.

Astute adults in positions to provide observationally based information may also be helpful to the child. This strategy calls for three groups of adults to work together.

9. Provide opportunities for gifted children to be together. This opportunity seems to alleviate some of the pressures a gifted child feels. For example, gifted students often report feeling different from other students, except when they have time to be together with other gifted students. When together, they often comment on the profound sense of relief of knowing there are other people like themselves who have many similar interests and qualities.

I hope you find some of these ideas helpful as you work on behalf of gifted children. The next chapters will continue this list of ideas to consider about the social and emotional needs of gifted students.

Practical Advice for Guiding the Gifted

T
he following was originally written to be the second installment in a three-part series on the social and emotional needs of gifted students. In the series, I broke with my past practice of trying to only forward ideas that have emerged from published research findings. Below are some ideas to consider as teachers, counselors, and parents attempt to guide the social and emotional development of gifted children.

1. Recognize and respect the relationship between social and emotional needs and academic needs. One affects the other. For example, whether a gifted student is challenged or able to work at a pace that is stimulating can affect his or her emotional well-being. Our school psychology clinic in Teachers College at Ball State University has documented that the most common reason gifted students are referred for psychological assessments is rooted in their becoming a behavior problem in school after having previously been a strong student.

The root of the behavioral change is the manifest frustration with not being challenged in school. For many students, this connection goes unnoticed until it is far too late to help them.

2. Be cautious about forcing your desires on students based on your perception of their strength areas. Talent manifests over time and with opportunity. Determining for a child what his or her "gift" or "talent" is without allowing for flexibility or encouraging additional self-exploration may cause a number of problems from adolescence on. A positive outcome of nurturing a talent is the development of a lifelong avocational interest or hobby.

3. Teach prosocial skill development. Teaching gifted students a handful of social skills can reduce the number of negative experiences they may encounter while in school. The phrasing of questions and comments and the ability to take another person's perspective are skills that are helpful in teaching gifted students to navigate the difficult social waters in schools.

4. Teach them to enjoy nonacademic activities. As appropriate, try to teach gifted students to recognize that nonacademic pursuits are also important in one's life. They become stress relievers and additional areas where gifted students can grow. Modeling works well in teaching this lesson.

5. Teach gifted students ways to manage stress. As they move through the grades, many will experience growing amounts of stress. Ironically, much of this will be self-imposed or a consequence of only their gift being recognized by those around them without concern for their needs as individuals. Because many gifted students develop coping strategies, educating them about how to effectively manage stress may prove relatively easy.

6. To accomplish many of the suggestions previously noted, adults should model the behavior they wish gifted students to exhibit. Like all children, gifted students learn

from the behavior of adults. Whether it is effective coping strategies, nonthreatening communication techniques, or how to relax, teachers, counselors, and parents often become the models that children follow. If you want your messages to be influential, let the students see you behaving accordingly.

7. Understand that much of how gifted students appear and behave is biologically affected. Do not try to change the basic nature of the student. Shyness, for example, like some physical characteristics, has roots in biology. Like the relationship between body type and weight, shyness and a student's willingness and ability to actively participate in class are related. Respect the nature of the individual gifted child.

8. Embrace diversity, do not merely tolerate it. To tolerate suggests a position of authority or position of judgment that allows someone to decide what human differences are meaningful and, therefore, acceptable and what differences are intolerable. This special privileged position tends to disadvantage gifted students because giftedness rarely makes people's lists of meaningful differences. As a teacher, parent, or counselor, you are in a position to have a significant impact on the minds of gifted children. If a school truly embraces diversity, then gifted students will be accepted. In many schools, giftedness is still experienced as being aberrant. In a study a few years ago, I found that gifted students are just as prone to believe stereotypical ideas about other gifted students as the general population. This phenomenon can be explained by the fact that gifted students cannot escape their environment.

9. Expose gifted students to knowledgeable counseling— avoid professionals who are not knowledgeable about gifted students. A proactive counseling program can be invaluable to gifted students. Learning about oneself and how to effectively relate to others in school can positively affect the psychological development of gifted students.

Conversely, messages learned from untrained counselors and psychologists who rely on intuition when providing services can actually exacerbate problems in the social and emotional realm.

10. Know that many gifted students will have created coping strategies while in the earliest grades in school. I have found that, by first grade, some gifted children have begun to engage in behavior patterns that reveal their discomfort with the gifted student label. Some of these strategies reflect their tacit knowledge about the social milieu of their classroom. Knowing that these patterns exist can enable teachers, counselors, and parents to understand the worries and behaviors surrounding gifted students' school experience.

11. Provide opportunities for down time. All children need time to relax away from school concerns. Arranging down time for some students will come easy, but for others it will be quite difficult. Providing gifted students opportunities to explore or read for pleasure can reduce stress and may have the positive effect of increasing avocational pursuits when they get older.

I hope you find some of these suggestions beneficial as you attempt to meet the social and emotional needs of gifted students. The next chapter will provide yet another list of considerations for parents, teachers and counselors as they attempt the important task of meeting the psychological, social, and emotional needs of gifted students.

Working on Behalf of Gifted Students

The following appeared as the third column in a series on meeting the social and emotional needs of gifted students. A number are somewhat specific to gifted students, while others might be as effective with students of average ability. Some of the ideas respect biological influences while others emphasize environmental influences in this area. Clearly, only some of the ideas expressed across the three-part series will be relevant for any specific student given his or her particular circumstances in life. Consequently, adults need to assess the salience of the ideas before attempting to pursue them.

1. Encourage controlled risk taking. Although it may seem on the surface to be an oxymoron, it really is not. Imagine the lives of professional stunt men and women. People who earn a living by risking their lives do so with careful planning. They take obvious risks to their physical well-being, but they do so after great effort has gone into building safety nets that minimize the potential for

their harm. Similarly, gifted students need to take risks to build same- and opposite-sex friendships and communicate with other students and teachers. To engage in this type of social risk taking, safeguards need to be in place. Parents, teachers, and counselors can create those safety nets with preparation. For example, building an accepting environment in a classroom and school establishes a climate that supports emotional and social risk taking. This suggestion dovetails into the next one.

2. Provide myriad social experiences for gifted students. In concert, the three groups of adults can orchestrate varied situations where gifted students interact with a wide variety of people. These types of experiences will build social skills specific to contexts and have the effect of developing the gifted students' social cognition. As the students have positive experiences, their self-concepts will also be enhanced.

3. Inventory family similarities and differences as compared to schoolmates. In some school settings, the diversity is obvious, while in others it is not. It can be helpful to gifted students for their parents, particularly, but also for teachers and counselors, to let them know what their family's values, practices, and beliefs are and how they vary across groups of people. If done within the context of diversity, then their giftedness can be accepted as quite normal, rather than aberrant.

4. To accomplish the previous suggestion, one approach is to encourage the reading of biographies of eminent people. This is considered a form of bibliotherapy. The details provided in the biographies will often cause two events to occur. The consciousness of the gifted student will be raised concerning the experiences the eminent person had that impacted his or her development. For example, some of the scientists in Germany prior to World War II speak about their lives as Jews during the rise of Hitler and the strong anti-Semitism that pervaded

Germany. The second event that often occurs is the combination of comparing the reader's life with that of the person in the biography, and then the awareness that many highly accomplished people also struggled with some of the same issues affecting the reader's life. This realization tends to reduce feelings of isolation while at the same time providing ideas for dealing with the difficulties gifted people encounter. Part of the potential effectiveness of the bibliotherapy approach is that the reader becomes actively engaged and creates his or her own understanding. This is a vastly different experience from having one's parent discuss issues with you. Although both reading biographies and discussing with parents can be successful, using both approaches may prove more beneficial than relying on only one.

5. A second approach for educating about diversity is to provide mentorship opportunities for gifted students. Apprenticeships can have many positive effects, including numerous ones in the skill-building domain. In this example, it is important to note the connection with the life story aspect of psychological development. For example, working with a mentor teaches many lessons, including who is the mentor and what pathway he or she followed to become what he or she is from the mentor's own perspective. Through this person's life story, salient issues in the individual development of the mentor can be recognized and understood by the gifted student. Like the effects of bibliotherapy, connecting with a significant adult who represents an academic area of interest to a gifted student offers many opportunities for the student to appreciate and navigate the social and emotional waters of his or her life.

6. Love and respect gifted students for who they are. Then, emphasize doing rather than being; ability and talent are neutral constructs, while doing is virtuous. Try to help them understand that being academically able does not

make a person good or bad, per se. Rather, like many characteristics one has, it is how one strives to develop and subsequently use other abilities that makes him or her virtuous. It is important for both gifted students and others to develop their talents. Avocational talent is important, too. The overemphasis by the three groups of adults on the students' abilities tends to create feelings by gifted students that they are nothing *but* their academic ability or achievement. This can lead to myriad problems, including underachievement, unnecessary suffering when doing poorly in school, the unwillingness to stretch beyond areas of prior attainment, and identity foreclosure. Identity foreclosure is the result of deciding at too young an age where to emphasize one's professional aspirations. Deciding to pursue math as a career because early in one's life a person is taught that he or she is particularly able in that area will often lead to the student choosing not to risk failure in other areas. Hence, other potential talent areas are never identified. Negative patterns within careers also exist for many who decided about their career too early in life.

7. Encourage a self-concept that extends far beyond the academic self-concept. It is never beneficial to a gifted student to convince him or her that only academic achievement is valuable. What good to society is a person who can calculate advanced math problems at an early age, but who has developed no civic responsibilities? Although I do not accept the claim that schools should attempt to develop equally the "whole" person, I do believe that gifted students should be appreciated as children who develop over time and, consequently, deserve the right to develop various aspects of their being. As in every preceding example, the three groups of adults need to work together for this suggestion to be realized.

Teachers, parents, and counselors should recognize the important roles they play in the psychological development of

gifted students. Gifted students will develop with or without adult guidance. The question is "How will they develop without coordinated guidance that is underpinned by research in developmental psychology and informed research on gifted students' lives in school?" My answer is that it is inconceivable that they can develop as well and as painlessly without the support of the three groups of adults. Let us commit to supporting the psychological development of all students, including gifted students.

Developing Relationships, Communication, and Identity

or this chapter, I have divided the suggestions that teachers, parents, and counselors can consider as they work on behalf of gifted students into four groups: (1) improving communication, (2) building relationships, (3) developing identity, and (4) for the adults. Many of the ideas are equally applicable to gifted students and students of average ability.

Improving Communication

One of the most effective approaches to improving the communication between gifted students and adults, and between gifted students and other students, is to encourage the expression of thoughts and feelings.

For many years, journaling has been used to elicit ideas and the exchange of thoughts and feelings between a teacher and student. It has also been used by therapists to gain insight into the client and to assist the client in the self-reflection process. The communication among both

groups (students/adults, students/other students) can be improved through journaling when the adult establishes goals for the student's journals and encourages the participation of the student.

A simple note of warning is called for here. Attempting to improve communication by reading a student's private journal (diary) will hurt rather than improve communication. The student is likely to feel violated by the adult, and he or she will most likely minimize communication for some period of time afterward.

Another way to improve communication is to create opportunities for the student to express him- or herself through artistic means. Again, this approach has a long, rich history in the field of psychology as a means of reaching difficult clients and in helping clients heal. I strongly encourage adults to use these techniques as stimuli only and not as diagnostic tools. The immediate benefit will be derived from the conversations enabled by the process and products, not due to any diagnosis made by the adult.

Building Relationships

The second set of suggestions is offered as a means to help gifted students build relationships with other people, both students and adults. Gifted students often feel that they have few friends with similar interests. Technological breakthroughs, particularly the use of electronic mail, has made communicating with others around the globe both immediate and inexpensive. I encourage the adults to look for ways to assist in the interactions of gifted students with others via e-mail.

This process is becoming increasingly common as teachers have their students create electronic pen pals as part of class assignments. These relationships are typically well-managed and quite safe for the students. Friendly relationships emerge as a natural consequence of gifted students meeting others like themselves. Tales abound of the friendships created during

specialized programs such as Governor's Schools or other summer residential programs that are sustained by using e-mail.

The more traditional approach of encouraging pen pal relationships still provides options for gifted students to build relationships with others who have similar interests. The traditional approach adds an additional level of safety, although it sacrifices the immediacy of using electronic mail. Both can work, but both need adult supervision.

In addition to developing relationships with other people, many benefits can be derived from involving the student with a pet. The relationship that often develops between children and pets is known to be very important in students' development of personal responsibility, compassion, and empathy. There can also be benefits from basic companionship.

Developing Identity

There are numerous ways of assisting in the development of a student's identity. Some are relatively easy to bring about, while others are much more difficult. Many adults may be unaware that gifted children often become concerned with ethical considerations of life at an earlier age than is common for most children. Adults are often surprised by the child's concerns, and sometimes they will make light of them. Anticipating and dealing honestly and empathetically with young children who are struggling with these worries can be very important to their development.

Gifted students should be encouraged to have an active life outside of school. There are benefits to outside activities that remain separate from school and those that have some connection to school. For example, learning to play musical instruments can originate in or out of school, and the potential transfer back and forth is generally a positive experience in building identity. Other parallel experiences include sports-related activities, such as soccer, baseball, football, and so forth. Sports, for those interested, can help develop a positive

sense of identity. I do, however, stress the need for the child to be interested. Few experiences are more difficult for children than to fail repeatedly in front of friends, family, and other people. Lack of interest, even when a student has ability, does not nurture skills development. This leaves them vulnerable to embarrassment.

A third suggestion is to respect the passions of the children, especially as they grow older. With young children, parents effectively control the children's activities. Consequently, the children tend to have options that are of some interest to their families.

As the students get older, they are allowed to explore more, potentially developing interests outside of their parents' desires. Balancing the time and energy needed to develop any area of endeavor is difficult. Parents need to allow the time for interests to develop, even when they are not the parents' interests. Respecting the passions of gifted students will assist in the development of their self-concepts and feelings of self-efficacy and agency.

A very important quality for healthy adults is empathy. Some gifted children have an abundance of empathy, while others need to be taught. Teaching empathy is not easy, but it can be done.

As noted in a previous chapter, helping develop a sophisticated understanding of human diversity can reduce the pain and suffering of gifted children as they realize that being different is both the norm and the exception; the norm in the infinite ways people differ, and the exception when one is seeking people who have similar interests, qualities, or beliefs.

Empathy for the lives of others enables gifted children to more fully appreciate that people have psychological needs that are similar to their own. Without empathy, gifted children can come to believe that they are completely estranged from others since the more obvious differences (e.g., academic passions) will dominate their perspectives of others.

One approach to developing empathy is to engage the child in an activity where each person assumes the perspective of another. Over time, the conditions can be changed so that difficult situations can be experienced vicariously to the extent necessary to build empathy.

For the Adults

The final category I have titled "for the adults." I include these suggestions because an unintended implication is that, if you follow the ideas outlined in this chapter, the gifted child will not suffer. As a psychologist, researcher, and parent, the hardest lesson I have had to learn is the inevitability of pain and suffering experienced by gifted children. This realization can elicit feelings of inadequacy and impotence in the adults around them.

I encourage the three groups of adults to work diligently to assist in the development of gifted children, but to be prepared for the difficulties of life. Constant communication can have a positive impact since many of life's difficulties will emerge from the child interacting in the adults' environments. Modeling calmness and caring may prove to be the best practice in which one can engage when the students are suffering with the normal trials and tribulations of life.

By being aware of the social and emotional needs of our young people, we will be better able to effectively guide their development. Let us continue to attempt to help all children enjoy rich and full lives, including gifted children.

Psychological Autopsy Provides Insight Into Gifted Adolescent Suicide

n the third chapter, "Examining Claims about Gifted Children and Suicide," I mentioned a study being conducted on the suicides of three gifted adolescents. That study appeared in a special issue of *The Journal of Secondary Gifted Education* (spring, 1996, vol. 7, no. 3). This chapter will highlight the findings of the study entitled "Psychological Autopsies of Three Academically Talented Adolescents Who Committed Suicide." I hope that the information will assist in the identification of gifted students who are at risk for suicidal behavior so that a reasoned intervention can take place.

Background Information

The three adolescent males in this study had attended a state-funded, residential high school for 280 academically talented 11th- and 12th- grade students in a midwestern state.

Research Methods

The psychological autopsy was designed to assess a variety of factors, including behaviors, thoughts, feelings, and relationships of an individual who is deceased (Ebert, 1987). It was originally developed as a means of resolving equivocal deaths and has expanded to include the analysis of nonequivocal suicides, with the intention of reducing their likelihood in similar groups of people (Jones, 1977; Neill, Benehsohn, Farber, & Resnick, 1974). It can be used as a posthumous evaluation of mental, social, and environmental influences on the suicide victim.

The psychological autopsy includes information from two areas: interviews with people who had significant relationships with the victim (e.g., parents, siblings, friends, teachers, romantic partners) and archival information related to the victim (e.g., school records, test information, medical records, personal letters, essays, diaries, suicide notes, artwork). Investigators analyze the information to identify themes and issues that may be valuable in the prediction of suicide within similar groups of people.

Results

The results have been organized into three categories: commonalities with adolescent suicide, commonalities among the three related to their giftedness, and themes that emerged across the three cases. The results have been excerpted with permission from the article "Psychological Autopsies of Three Academically Talented Adolescents Who Committed Suicide" by Cross, Cook, and Dixon (1996).

Commonalities with Adolescent Suicide in the General Population

1. All subjects were adolescent Caucasian males.

2. They each manifest four emotional commonalities:
   - depression,
   - anger,
   - mood swings, and
   - confusion about the future.
3. They each manifest three behavioral commonalities:
   - poor impulse control,
   - substance use and abuse, and
   - extensive journaling.
4. They each manifest four relational commonalities:
   - romantic relationship difficulties,
   - self-esteem difficulties (either by exaggeration or self-condemnation),
   - conflictual family relationships, and
   - isolation from persons capable of disconfirming irrational logic.
5. The subjects shared warning signs in six categories:
   - behavior problems,
   - period of escalation of problems,
   - constriction (withdrawal, friends, dichotomous thinking, talk of suicide),
   - talking about suicide,
   - changes in school performance, and
   - family histories of psychological problems.

Commonalities Among the Three Cases Related to Their Giftedness

1. The subjects exhibited overexcitabilities:
   - Expressed in ways or levels beyond the norm even among their gifted peers.
   - Had minimal prosocial outlets.
   - Experienced difficulty separating fact from fiction, especially overidentification with negative asocial or aggressive characters or themes in books and movies.
   - Experienced intense emotions.

- Felt conflicted, pained, and confused.
- Devalued emotional experience, except for pain.
2. They each expressed polarized, hierarchical, egocentric value systems.
3. They each engaged in group discussions of suicide as a viable and honorable solution.
4. They each expressed behavior consistent with Dabrowski's Level II or Level III of Positive Disintegration.
5. They each attended residential school as a means of escape (family, hometown).

Themes Emerging Across the Three Cases

1. All three suffered from depression: Case 1 was hospitalized for depression; Case 2 was a classic marked depression (his journal clearly reflects the depressive thought of negative view of self, negative view of the future); and Case 3 was identified as in need of treatment by school personnel, and his journal reflects clinical depression.
2. Suicide contagion seemed to have been operative: Case 3 seemed particularly to follow Case 2, while Case 1 set the stage for discussion of suicide, and the suicide of the musical group Nirvana's lead singer, Kurt Cobain, was related.
3. Suicide has a cultural component: music (e.g., Nirvana, Jane's Addiction, Sex Pistols), literature (e.g., Anne Rice, H. P. Lovecraft), and movies (e.g., *Heathers*) all played important parts for these adolescents. Even though many teenagers may consume similar media, there seemed to be an excessive focus on dark, negative content.
4. They had many characteristics identified as overexcitabilities (e.g., very sensitive, two were vegetarians, fantasy, mixing truth and fiction).
5. Suicide has a social component. The topic of suicide was openly discussed among the students in their peer groups; their discussions reduced the taboo associated with suicide and supported their position that suicide is a free choice

that was their decision to make. As a result, there was no need to seek help or make referrals.

6. Excessive introspection and obsessive thinking was evident. The journals served as ways to avoid interaction with others, and, as a result, irrational thinking fed itself rather than being disconfirmed by others.

7. The issue of control over others was present in two cases. This control resulted in attempts to harm in one case.

Unanswered Questions

The following is a list of questions that remain largely unanswered at the end of the study.

1. How large a role does suicide contagion play in multiple suicides?

2. What role does unsupervised journaling play in suicide?

3. What is the extent of influence that overexcitabilities play in suicide ideation and behavior?

4. Does exploring dark issues by this age group make them vulnerable to suicide?

5. What is the effect on suicide behavior of residential schools aggregating students with similar high-risk factors (e.g., previous suicide ideation or attempts) in a setting that encourages self-exploration?

6. What role does the combination of asynchronous development and dark literature play in suicide ideation?

7. What role does the lack of religious beliefs have on suicide behavior?

8. What is the influence of popular cultural icons who commit suicide on suicide behavior of gifted adolescents?

9. What effect does believing suicide is an honorable option have on suicide behavior?

10. What is the role that popular media, where violence (including suicide and homicide) are pervasive, have on suicide behavior?

I offer these suggestions for you to consider as you think about the social and emotional needs of gifted children. You are cautioned to remember that the results were based on only three cases and, therefore, may not be representative of the larger phenomenon.

Recommendations for Preventing the Suicides of Gifted Adolescents

1. Keep an eye out for:
   - emotional difficulties, especially anger or depression;
   - lack of prosocial activities;
   - dissatisfaction with place, situation, school, peers, family, or self;
   - difficulties in romantic relationships, especially with peers of similar abilities;
   - non-normative expression of overexcitabilities, especially unbalanced expression of overexcitabilities (predominantly negative, asocial, or antisocial); and
   - difficulty separating fact from fiction (overidentification with characters, especially antiheroes and aggressive characters).
2. Err on the side of caution.
   - Do not overlook potential signs of suicide just because the child is gifted.
   - Accept the uniqueness of gifted adolescents, but not at the risk of overlooking indicators of emotional, psychological, or suicidal distress.
3. Be proactive.
   - Educate gifted adolescents about their emotional experiences and needs.
   - Communicate, communicate, communicate.
   - Challenge the idea that suicide is an honorable solution.
   - Strive for a balance of positive and negative themes and characters in curricula, books, and audiovisual materials.

- Assess for emotional, psychological, and relational difficulties.
- When in doubt, do something!

Gifted Children Today

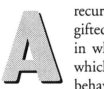

A recurring theme in my efforts to learn more about gifted children is the difference between the times in which they are growing up and the times in which I grew up. As I have tried to evaluate their behavior and their social and emotional needs, it comes up again and again. AIDS, MTV, guns in school, the Internet—all of these impact the lives of gifted children. This theme is the foundation for the three chapters in this section.

I introduce these ideas in "Gifted Students' Social and Emotional Development in the 21st Century." Rollo May's notion that we cannot truly understand something until we have experienced it serves as a reminder to us all that we must delve ever more deeply into the psyche of young people if we want to help them succeed in these new, very different times. The tragic incident at Columbine High School in April of 1999 is a most potent indicator of the different times in which these children are growing up. How giftedness plays a role in their experience is the emphasis of the column titled "The Lived Experiences of Gifted Students in School or On Gifted Students and Columbine." Building on the concepts discussed in the first section (About Gifted Children: Who They Are and Why), this column explores misconceptions about gifted children and how they interact with these new times to make an even more complicated world for gifted young people.

The work of Margaret Mead, anthropologist *extraordinaire*, provides a foundation for a further look into our "Changing Times." Anthropological studies of cultural change reveal the complexity of our current state. We are all pioneers, the youth among us even more than the adults. As we work to help them find their way, we must learn about the influences unique to our time.

Gifted Students' Social and Emotional Development in the 21st Century

The complications involved in raising children increased significantly during the second half of the 20th century. Charles Dickens' quote "It was the best of times, it was the worst of times" seems an apt statement to describe the societal changes since 1960. These changes have been so dramatic and pervasive that they are, in fact, hard to fully comprehend. The last 40 years have seen many changes, from what were once considered global issues, such as population growth and environmental concerns (seemingly so distant and unrelated to us living in the United States 40 years ago), to the daily activities in which we each engage. As we guide the youth of today, we must consider both the broad and specific contexts of our children's times. In the last 40 years, we have moved from only three available television channels to literally hundreds, from curable types of venereal diseases to herpes and AIDS, from 16k of computer memory to terabytes at roughly the same cost, letter writing to e-mail, and the world's population has grown from three billion to six billion people.

Given the important ways in which our world has changed and will continue to change, those of us from earlier generations need to appreciate that we can only know *about* what it is like to be growing up gifted in the new millennium. Despite the breadth and depth of the changes, one might argue that small-town life has not changed much over the past 40 years. While this can be a true statement, I would note that MTV is one example of how a generation has been connected through image and sound unlike all previous generations. This one simple example brings to bear all the considerations associated with psychosocial development. For example, historically, as a young child moved from parents being the ones with the greatest influence on his or her immediate behavior to friends being more influential, the small groups of friends tended to carefully reflect the child's immediate communities in terms of values, appearance, and comportment. Via MTV and other similar channels, young people of today make a visual and auditory connection with youth throughout the United States. Consequently, the reference groups of youth are no longer so closely tied to immediate communities. Issues such as fitting in, developing a peer group, understanding one's role in his or her family and the broader culture are but a few of the issues that emerge as potentially influencing the needs of gifted children. All these concerns and experiences occur as children are forming their identities.

The following are two examples of ways that children's experiences vary significantly from previous generations and illustrate meaningful variations within the past 20 years.

Schooling Practices
- from textbooks and worksheets to computers
- from teacher-directed to students as teachers
- from lecturing to students becoming responsible for the construction of their own learning through processes of inquiry

Access to Information
- from slow and sometimes unattainable to immediate and overwhelming
- from being out in the world collecting information to collecting information from home
- from collecting information manually to relying on computers

As adults, we must realize that, while we try to understand our children's lives, in many important ways they are unlike our own. A famous psychologist, Rollo May (1969), wrote that we must recognize the difference between knowing about something and truly knowing something. May described how he came down with tuberculosis and was on his deathbed. He dealt with the salient aspects and issues of preparing for death. He recovered and came to realize that, before this experience, he only knew about death. After having experienced the life of a dying person, he truly knew death. To know something, one must experience it. Most of our lives are spent merely knowing about things. As newborns, we learn in a prelingual manner largely determined by our parents until our mobility allows for our own experimentation. Even with trial and error experiences, we are being taught to learn vicariously by watching and listening to others. We also learn how to create and understand the world as mental activities without relying on others' input or examples.

Much of what we come to know about and believe comes from our environmental teachings and mental constructions, and far less through our own experiments. This distinction is important for many reasons. The first is that no two people can have the exact same understanding of any situation or construct. Another is that historical analysis has taught us that cohorts in history often reveal patterns of thought and value formations that are similar. For example, in the United States, the young adult population living during the Watergate scandal has maintained a level and type of political skepticism dif-

ferent from the young adults of the Reagan era. A third is that, along with the acceleration of technological advances over the past 40 years, there has been tremendous growth in the knowledge of virtually all subjects. Various means, such as the Internet and personal computers, now provide access to the expanding information base in increasingly easier and faster ways. There now exists a "digital divide," a serious and expanding gap between the knowledge, opportunities, and wealth of those in the world who have regular and easy access and those who have neither. The relationship between young children's access to self-selected material and their social and emotional development has yet to be studied. Therefore, it is difficult to predict the effects on typical development patterns of the immediate access to and consumption of material that cuts across topics and age appropriateness.

Another major confluence of events that are radically changing current experiences (and hence all that is affected by them) is the movement to a world economy. Opportunities and expectations are becoming influenced by what is and is not perceived as possible. For example, many Indiana natives who grew up between the 1950s and the 1980s aspired to and relied on manufacturing jobs upon graduation from high school. This possibility allowed families to remain physically close and often work together. In recent years, however, the move to a world economy has drained the manufacturing jobs that defined the state's economy. Despite the fact that the state has relatively low unemployment rates of 4–5%, the adult population is often underemployed and earns a fourth to a third of previous incomes, while their children grapple with giving up on their aspirations. This evolution is slow and often painful. More importantly, these changes are being played out on a world stage where being a consumer is characterized as being a good citizen.

As concerned adults interested in helping the psychosocial development of gifted students, we should first heed Rollo May's words: To truly know and understand another's experi-

ences, we must live them ourselves. Secondly, we should maintain a healthy respect for those experiences that are consistent across generations and those that are not. We must be aware of the differences in children's experiences and in our own. With our new appreciation for the profound differences of experience as compared to our children, we should draw on all resources available to assist the children in question. It would also be helpful for adults to learn some basic theory about human development, particularly as it pertains to the psychosocial development of gifted students. There are certain aspects of human development theory that are resistant to change over time.

By realizing our limitations in being truly empathetic and by utilizing the strategies noted, we have the opportunity to provide effective guidance to the gifted youth of the 21st century. I am sure that Rollo May, by asking us to experience another's suffering in order to know it, never meant to encourage the pain and suffering of even one additional person in order to widen expertise in the face of any specific tragedy. I am quite confident that he would have advised us to operate in a climate of trust and with an appreciation for the child's experiences as being meaningful and valid. Our role should, therefore, be one of compassion and respect for the uniqueness of all gifted children as they struggle with the development of their identity while on the path to self-actualization.

The Lived Experiences of Gifted Students in School, or On Gifted Students and Columbine

T he purpose of this chapter is to create a context for understanding gifted students' lives in school. To that end, I will highlight how gifted students deal with the mixed messages they perceive from their environment and try to make a connection with the recent tragedy at Columbine High School. While the topic is quite somber, there is ultimately good news to be shared about gifted students' lives.

Since the middle 1980s, Larry Coleman, and I have been publishing research about the lives of gifted students in school (e.g., Coleman & Cross, 1988; Cross, Coleman, & Terhaar-Yonkers, 1991). Data for some of the early articles published on this topic were collected during evaluations of schools and programs for gifted students. During the early evaluations (circa 1984), the gifted students described in great detail what their lives in their local schools were "really like." The "really like" aspect of their comments inspired us to approach the research in a more serious, deliberate, and focused manner. Since then Larry and I, individually and in

tandem, have gathered data from thousands of gifted students in grades K–12 from numerous states across the nation. We have used surveys and questionnaires; made observations; interviewed students, teachers, parents, and administrators; visited numerous schools and classrooms; and read students' journals all in the quest of understanding gifted students' lives in school. Over the past 15 years, we have published approximately 20 articles and presented more than 40 papers together at conferences dealing with gifted students. The research has led me to my ideas about the shootings at Columbine. This chapter will provide ideas that were developed while working on the various studies previously reported. In addition to this line of research, I have increasingly focused on the psychology of gifted students, with a specialization in the suicidal behaviors of gifted students. Our research into the social and emotional development of gifted students, their experiences of giftedness, their social cognition, and their social coping strategies and behaviors have also informed this chapter.

For 20 years, I have claimed that schools are first and foremost a social enterprise where some academic learning goes on. While I have used this statement to frame my social-cognitive orientation, the original idea emerged during an interview with a gifted adolescent who was describing to me his life as a student. The detail reflected in his perceptions about the expectations within his numerous school placements was most impressive. He also described expectations from outside his school that reflect messages society held about gifted students. The degree to which the messages were mixed was quite astonishing to me. For example, he perceived that gifted students are physically weak, socially inadequate, and not interesting people. They are out of touch, unattractive, and have a high propensity for mental problems. While the student knew that many of these descriptors did not fit him, he had come to believe that being gifted was somewhat limiting. Another important message he received was that going to college was important. To go to college, one needs to work hard as a stu-

dent. He also believed that pursuing excellence was important in life. For example, "do your best" was described as the single most frequent comment from adults. Across these various messages was a thread that established implicit parameters on his behavior that was different than the messages. The thread was interpreted as *not too*. Study hard, but *not too* hard. Pursue academic passions, but *not too* much. Even do your best in school, but *not* if it means spending *too* much time or energy to do so. Increasingly, the understood message was that, to be a healthy person, one spreads time spent in activities across a variety of endeavors that seem reasonable to adults. A secondary message inferred from these mixed messages was that being gifted should not take so much of your time or, said differently, if one must spend so much time on his or her academic studies, then he or she must not be gifted.

Over the years, I have heard other beliefs held by many gifted students that pertain to these mixed messages. Three of the most common are that others hold expectations about gifted students; that if one becomes known as a gifted student, it affects how others treat him or her; and that one learns that if he or she can manage the information others gain about him or her, then he or she can maintain a more social latitude. This information management system becomes the means gifted students use to navigate the social expectations and the mixed messages society holds about them. These three beliefs are called the Stigma of Giftedness Paradigm (SGP; Coleman, 1985). The SGP has been studied for years and found to be a good way to understand and explain gifted students' experience in school settings. The social cognition and coping strategies are also explained by this understanding of the basic SGP.

Recently, some important writings have attempted to compare and contrast the developmental patterns of gifted students by comparing them to patterns of typical development. Some of the more idiosyncratic patterns of development are also being explored. By the latter, I mean the development of gifted students that reflects their own emerg-

ing biologically determined qualities, natural developmental tendencies, environmental opportunities, their own agency, and specific opportunities to develop in areas not typical for others. This area of study will require decades of exploration. For now, I think that, in order to understand the lives of gifted students, it is important to note one's time in history, large societal influences, more localized social expectations, and specific patterns of influence on gifted children.

An important finding in an early study was that young gifted students perceive expectations and societal messages through the eyes of an immature mind. Because their social and emotional development is often more age-appropriate than their academic abilities, consideration of the early perceptions of mixed messages on their development needs serious ongoing study.

What can we say about gifted students' experiences in school? They receive mixed messages. Some messages are at the macrolevel, while others are at the microlevel. Others are internal to the individual. They try to understand and live within the messages they receive. They develop social-coping strategies to blend in with their environments to the extent they desire. Gifted students experience the same societal influences as their cohort. For example, access to weapons, suicidal patterns, and familial problems or issues (e.g., divorce rates) also impact them. All these influences are also affected by friendships and idiosyncratic qualities of the individual. For example, an individual's level of mental health is a key ingredient to both his or her experiences in school and his or her behaviors.

All these influences bring us to the recent shootings of students at Columbine High School in Littleton, CO. Before I comment specifically on that event, I want to add to the equation a few other influences that were important, yet rarely discussed. All students are forced by law to be in the presence of other students for several hours a day in close proximity. Teachers typically have their time dedicated to specific tasks

that direct their time and energy to certain settings. What emerge are behaviors from the students that society either allows or does not actively discourage. For example, some adults assume that, in school, students bully each other and girls need to learn how to be able to turn away those who harass them. From a sociological perspective, I assert that a society's prejudices are allowed to exist within schools. Racism, sexism, classism, and so forth are present and active in most schools. The fact that these exist in school is not meant to be a criticism of teachers. I have a great deal of respect for teachers as the individuals who often end or prevent these problems. We can take as an example of the rampant prejudice held by students two groups who have for years been subjected to numerous types of assaults: gay and lesbian students. These two groups illustrate how difficult it is to exist in these microcosms of society we call schools. When the mixed messages that gifted students experience are factored in with the extent to which other prejudices manifest themselves in schools, it is quite amazing to me that gifted kids tend to be as well adjusted as they are.

Several parents of gifted students have told me that their children have surprised them by saying that, while they do not condone the shooting of other students at Columbine, they can understand the feelings of rage that go along with being tormented in school. These parents drew on their own experiences to conclude that trials and tribulations—vis-à-vis bullying and harassment—of students today are the same as those they had as children. Students' experiences in school today are somewhat similar to and somewhat different from the experiences of previous generations. How they are the same is important, and how they are different is very important. Children should feel safe while in school. They cannot thrive when they feel threatened. They grow up in environments knowing anyone who gets mad at them can easily access a gun. Their antagonist may even have the gun with them while at school. Even those few people from previous generations who

did have similar worries would not have had to seriously consider the possibility of contending with automatic weapons or pipe bombs.

The final factor I believe to be pertinent to the lived experience of gifted students is that the beliefs learned adults hold about gifted students are often tacit to them. They only come to realize what they believe when faced with events or circumstances that bring to the surface their actual beliefs or feelings. For example, a few years ago a sophisticated reporter for the *Chicago Tribune* interviewed me about Theodore Kaczynski, the "Unabomber." The reporter had worked for weeks putting together a story about Kaczynski's history that emphasized the fact that he was a gifted student. Several leaders in the field of gifted education were interviewed. The reporter asked me, "Did Ted Kaczynski commit murder because he was allowed to skip two grades in school?" What an amazing assumption! Does accelerating gifted students cause them to become serial killers? My response was, "I hope not, because tens of thousands of students are grade-skipped each year." I was stunned to learn that such an educated person could hold such foolish misconceptions. Imagine what messages are sent to gifted students by less well-educated or academically oriented people. Also imagine how gifted students are actually treated if large numbers of adults, including well-educated adults, hold such wild misconceptions about them.

Putting the Pieces Together

Gifted students need adults to guide them. They need adults who understand them to help them develop with few limitations. Although patterns and trends among people can be understood at the macrolevel, acts of individuals must be understood at the individual level. The students at Columbine who murdered their classmates have been described in the press as gifted students. The lesson of Columbine is not that gifted students are homicidal; rather, the lesson is that the chil-

dren who killed other students had certain qualities, histories, and experiences. They had access to lethal weapons and the time to plan the killings. Their giftedness should in no way be assumed as a cause agent in their inappropriate act. Their behavior has become a mirror for society's prejudice. A lesson of Columbine should be that schools must create safe environments where learning can thrive. Larger issues like the relationship between the size of schools and the social milieu should be considered. Our research has suggested that being gifted in differing types of school settings leads to different experiences.

Another important question should be, "What size or configuration of school allows for optimal relationships to be forged among students, between students and teachers, and students and guidance counselors?" Few professionals who work in or with public schools believe that we are able to create optimal educational settings. We seem destined to work with what we have. For example, some high schools are so large that their school counselors rarely get to know the students for whom they are responsible. In Indiana, the ratio of high school students to school counselors often exceeds 400 to 1. This speaks to the extent to which schools are not effectively designed to prevent incidents like the one at Columbine. Rather than finding easy, quick condemnations for gifted students, we must commit ourselves to helping all students thrive, including gifted students.

Looking for ways to create positive environments in which all of these students can coexist and actually thrive should be a goal of our society. Blaming schools, television violence, video violence, or divorce rates for the events at Columbine are superficial and will only lead to band-aid approaches to long-term complicated problems. While I am troubled about the deaths of the victims at Columbine, I am hoping that Americans will recognize that our culture tolerates the abuse of disempowered students in certain ways and to such a degree that it requires a rare event to bring it to the surface. Let us

take the opportunity during this time of our country's financial boom to reconfigure the support resources needed to guide our students to healthy lives. Columbine was a rare event that could be looked back on as the event that raised our country's consciousness about the need to create safe, nurturing environments in our schools.

Changing
Times

n a previous chapter, "Gifted Students' Social and Emotional Development in the 21st Century," I attempted to illustrate some of the salient ways in which the lives of gifted students today are significantly different from previous generations. Later in that chapter, I made a plea to adults to understand that growing up in a time not experienced by previous generations requires us to act in ways that are not necessarily the ways we think we should. In this chapter, I continue the theme by drawing on the works of the very famous anthropologist Margaret Mead, as well as from some less well-known contemporary authors.

As a researcher interested in how we can guide gifted children's development in the psychological realm to help them become as healthy, happy, and successful as possible, I often read other scholars' accounts of where we are as a nation and world, where we have been, and where we are going. From my readings, I try to select the meaningful from the less meaningful. I have come to believe in a few of

what I consider relatively stable factors, some variables that are in transition, and some important variables that are changing rapidly in important ways.

The first rather stable factor is that the United States is made up of a large number of cities, towns, and hamlets, with untold numbers of ghettos, communities, and villages. Across this array of living conditions are the myriad other ways people vary (e.g., ethnically, racially, religiously, regionally). Hence, when we think of the lives of our gifted students, we have to acknowledge that there is no one United States per se, but instead we have hundreds of differing influences factoring into the specifics of the lived experience of being gifted as an American. The specifics of the experience can be put under a loose interpretation of the notion of the culture in which a person lives.

An example of an important convention cutting across the enormous variation in the United States that has significant impact on gifted children's lives (perhaps not equally, however) is the institution of marriage. At the same time as the change in the divorce rate in the U.S., there has also appeared a change in the manifestations of the nuclear family that includes increasing numbers of hybrid families and single-parent homes. There are some obvious and some less-obvious outcomes of these types of changes on the psychological well-being of gifted students.

The next important factor is an example of one in transition. I include Mead's description of how our society has been evolving over the past generations. In 1970, Margaret Mead described a new cultural trend born of the technological changes of the past century. She noted that early cultures were easily transmitted from generation to generation because individuals always lived close to home. Three generations—children, parents, and grandparents—existed together in the same place. She called this a *postfigurative* culture, and in it a child's life would be predictably like his or her grandparents'. As travel increased and young people moved away from their

families, children's lives no longer mirrored their grandparents' lives, so the young people looked to their peers or other adults for cultural definition. Therefore, according to Mead, in this *cofigurative* culture, young people rely on the experience of their elders to a point; but, after that, they must learn from the members of their new place how to fit in. Mead claims that advances in technology have made Americans immigrants both in place, as we have become a transient society, and in time, as our world has changed so rapidly through technology. Hence, our new *prefigurative* culture must create its own society without a dependence on the experiences of our elders. Mead described an erroneous assumption adults often hold about their and subsequent generations:

> It is assumed by the adult generation that there still is general agreement about the good, the true, and the beautiful and that human nature, complete with built-in ways of perceiving, thinking, feeling, and acting, is essentially constant. Such beliefs are, of course, wholly incompatible with a full appreciation of the findings of anthropology, which has documented the fact that innovations in technology and in the form of institutions inevitably bring about alterations in cultural character. It is astonishing to see how readily a belief in change can be integrated with a belief in changelessness, even in cultures whose members have access to voluminous historical records and who agree that history consists not merely of currently desirable constructs but of verifiable facts. (p. 60)

The third category of factors that are important and changing very rapidly continues from Mead's quote. The growth of the personal computer, generally, and the emergence of the Internet, specifically, are illustrating an important example of what Mead claimed over 30 years ago: "innovations in technology and in the form of institutions inevitably

bring about alterations in cultural character" (p. 60). An early example of this type of effect can be found in the South. Numerous books have been written about Southern hospitality, particularly as it pertains to impromptu social interactions on sidewalks, porches, streets, and the like. Where people crossed paths, a gracious interaction took place. With the new technology of air conditioning came many fewer outdoor interactions of both strangers and friends alike. The effect of two generations having grown up with air conditioning has changed some of the cultural expectations for what it is to be Southern. Over time, these cultural expectations will be lost, to a large extent because of the effects of technology.

A more contemporary example of technology affecting our culture is still relatively early in its development. It is the overall effect of relying on computers for several types of activities that have typically required social interactions among various groups of people. Arguably, the most developed of these types of activities is the purchasing of products or services using the Internet. The most noticeable aspect of the development of the Internet over the past five years has been its commercialization. Monumental efforts to make available all types of products for purchase have seemingly driven the development of the Internet. Everything from automobiles to opportunities to gamble can be purchased while sitting in one's home. These are ingredients for cultural change: opportunity, control, anonymity, and convenience. In a recent lecture, software engineer and author Ellen Ullman described the marketing term *disintermediation* as a goal for businesses intent on using the Internet to separate the purchaser from everything except what is being bought (2000). Disintermediation establishes the single consumer sitting at home, often alone, as the most powerful force in purchasing. To accomplish this goal, advertisers have marketed such concepts as this one found on the billboard of the San Francisco theater: "Now the world really does revolve around you." Ullman went on to claim that the effects of this technology and marketing over time pro-

motes the "my" mentality in a very powerful way: "the 'My Computer' icon bothers me on the Windows desktop, baby names like 'My Yahoo' and 'My Snap'; my, my, my; two-year-old talk; infantilizing and condescending" (p. 31). Advertising slogans such as "Wouldn't you rather be at home?" along with the rapid advancements in technology have been projected to lead to a total individuation of experiences. For example, Ullman cited a museum owner's comments that soon extensive art holdings accessible through the Internet will lead to people establishing exhibits only representing their personal interests. His example, "Today I visited the museum of me. I liked it," is indicative of the wave about to affect our society.

Innumerable outcomes will potentially come from this shifting to the individual as the most valued. Two are the idea that civil space will no longer be needed and that the only place of pleasure and satisfaction is your home. As adults needing to guide gifted children, we must appreciate the substantial diversity making up the United States, understand the changes in the family structures in ways that honor the natural diversity that comes from cultural evolution, and learn what we can in the general arena of technology. From this wisdom we should be able to accommodate the ever-changing social and emotional needs of all children, including gifted children.

Where We
Have Been
and
Where We
are Going

his section of the book contains only one piece entitled "Top Ten (plus or minus two) List for the 20th
Century." This was not one of my regular columns.
For the end-of-the-millenium issue of *Gifted Child
Today*, several professionals in the field of gifted education
were asked to overview what they believed were the most
important events that occurred over the past century, with an
eye on predicting the future of the field. The ideas conveyed
represent my way of thinking, which tends to emphasize connections while trying to understand historical patterns. I also
tend to believe that sociopolitical forces influence many of the
important trends in educational policy and practice.

Top Ten (plus or minus two) List for the 20th Century

T he following represents ideas about some of the most influential events, circumstances, or decisions to affect gifted education over the past 100 years. Some of the events are well known, while others may not be known at all. Some of the circumstances reflect the world according to Tracy, while others are quite possibly part of history that has been, or one day will be written about. Some of the decisions represent my take on them and may be arguable as facts, while others may represent a consensus in the field. In short, the ideas expressed here may not represent the folks at *GCT*, Prufrock Press, or any other living, breathing person. They have been fun to think about, and the process has helped me clarify some of the underpinnings on which I base other ideas. While I doubt that this list will become a historical road map for the field of gifted education, I hope it becomes the impetus for others to ponder this subject.

One of the assumptions I operated under while working on my list was that, because I knew that a couple of very

capable thinkers were working on the same assignment, there would probably be some overlap in our lists. Consequently, I used that assumption to take some liberties with the charge. In a final prefacing comment, I would like to note that, once given this assignment by Dr. Susan Johnsen, I started generating items for top ten lists. I worked on this by carrying around a pad and pencil for a couple of months. To date, I have created 14 different top ten lists. I even lost one. A few of the lists were created as I woke up in the middle of the night having had what I thought at the time was an epiphany. Several of those lists were ripped to shreds, burned, then buried. So much for the creativity of my unconscious mind. This list is really an amalgam of ideas that seemed to reappear across the numerous lists generated, or seemed to reflect ideas that might not get me drummed out of the field if I actually wrote them down. To make my thinking understandable in an efficient manner, I will tie together ideas that I believe are indicators and/or examples of the point I am trying to make. By explaining them, they may appear to be discrete from each other. In many cases, however, the ideas are connected, and in some cases, one idea sets the stage for the next, not necessarily in a planned way, but more like the ways in which ideas are shown to lead to others on the PBS series *Connections*. One final wringing of hands: My way of thinking is highly contextually driven. Consequently, the ideas will not be as detailed as I tend to imagine them.

Rather than count down from ten to one, I will offer a set of ten (or so), starting with events in the late 1800s. I will call this set of events "From the Apgar score to the Licensing Exam," or "The Reign of Standardized Testing." Better yet, number 10 is the emergence of efficient ways for making important educational decisions. Let me use the phrase *psychometrically based pedagogy*. I will credit the development of the Binet intelligence test as the earliest influence. From Binet came the Army Alpha and Beta tests, the Stanford Binet, Wechsler series and a host of other efforts to measure a per-

son's intellectual ability (and everything else about them, as well). The efficiency of group intelligence tests allowed decisions to be made in a highly time-efficient manner that, in my mind, set the standard for high-stakes testing. For example, doing poorly on the Army tests increased one's chances of going to the front during World War I as a foot soldier, where they died at a higher rate than those in other positions. The attitude was created, or at least reflected, in these practices that psychometric principles should be the basis for making hard decisions about young people's roles and responsibilities in the United States. From this period emerged the original Terman (1925) studies on intelligence. His work reflected the science and views of people of the era, yielding arguably the single most important study underpinning the field of gifted education today. While it is unfair and anachronistic to hold Terman's research to all the considerations and criteria of research conducted today, it is a fair statement that some in the field of gifted education have determined that the Terman research is quite limited in its representation of the many conceptions of giftedness that are popular today. Even with these concerns, I believe that the influence of the Terman research on today's ideas of giftedness cannot be overestimated. The research also added support for the use of standardized intelligence tests and to the conception of giftedness described in the studies. Moreover, the term IQ has become so ingrained in the American vernacular and psyche, that groups of adults belong to clubs based on their IQ test score. The last name of Albert Einstein has become synonymous with a high IQ score. "He's no Einstein" is a criticism often used to describe people thought to be dull.

During this time in history, Sigmund Freud was quite prominent in influencing beliefs about the nature of people. While his views are both interesting and insightful, they did little to help the relatively young public school system accommodate the increasing numbers of immigrant children needing, expecting, and being forced to participate in schooling.

Fortunately for the schools, John Watson and Edward Thorndike were setting the stage for Fred (a.k.a. B. F.) Skinner to provide some of the underpinnings needed to educate vast numbers of children from modest means. Skinner, Thorndike, and other behaviorists reified the concepts of a type of psychology and became the architects of mass schooling. While Terman's influence helped establish an entity notion of giftedness—that giftedness is a thing that can be measured—the behaviorists influenced later writers to think that looking at the behaviors of children is a more important concern than relying on paper- and pencil-tests. The behaviorist view of teaching and learning required teachers to teach from the smallest concept to the larger idea by chaining. More importantly, however, behaviorists' mechanistic views of humankind challenged our basic core beliefs about people. Behaviors are learned; therefore, giftedness can be influenced. With these ideas, the early seeds were sown to add environmental influences to our prevailing concept of genius. Clearly, despite the fact that early philosophers had already espoused both positions, their influence was not so great as the philosopher psychologists in the first half of the 20th century.

In 1957, the Russians launched Sputnik. From all accounts, this event led the United States to begin an aggressive effort to catch up with the Russians in the space race. Of course, the Cold War and the fear that the Russians would dominate the world fueled this race. From this single event, numerous national, state, and local efforts to better prepare students in math and science were begun. For several years, educating students in mathematical and scientific areas seemed to be a high priority for the U.S. Prior to this period and for many years following, Albert Einstein was one of the most recognized and respected people in the world. His popularity was that of a celebrity—the Michael Jordan of the era. Children aspired to be like Einstein.

In the 1960s, a cultural and civil rights revolution was in full force. From fashion, to political attitudes, to one's very

personal aspirations, ideals were changing. Dr. Martin Luther King Jr., Rosa Parks, and many others sought to bring to all people the same opportunities as those enjoyed by the people who had maintained power since the early years of the country. The Civil Rights Law, passed in 1964, signaled what I believe to be one of the three most important influences on gifted education. While it is hard to imagine, prior to 1964, and, to some extent, today, children of color have been left out of educational efforts to maximize talent.

The next event that has had a significant impact on gifted education was the passage of Public Law 94–142 in 1974. This law effectively required schools to provide appropriate educational services to students with disabilities. When one reviews the history of public schools in the United States, few single events have had more impact on the overall practices of schools throughout the U.S. than this law. While I am somewhat disappointed that gifted students did not become a direct part of this law as a protected group, I believe that the law's influence on the American understanding of education and the responsibility we have to accommodate the needs of exceptional students did have a tremendous impact on the lives of gifted students.

Between 1974 and today, one topic (conceptions of intelligence) has been widely written about both in the popular press and scholarly journals. The articles have had a tremendous impact on educators' thinking and, to a large extent, have pushed along our notions of giftedness. While many of the contemporary notions of giftedness are not limited to an intelligence-based foundation, the field of gifted education is both underpinned by it and somewhat held hostage to populists' notions of intelligence. In 1983, the book *Frames of Mind* by Howard Gardner was published. Soon thereafter, another view of intelligence by Robert Sternberg was published. Since the mid-1980s, numerous views have emerged. This public debate has been broad, with public school educators leading the way. It was clear that our traditional IQ-based

notion of intelligence was too narrow to reflect the experiences of our nation's educators. Nothing was more powerful that an idea whose time had come. In essence, teachers were rejecting many psychologists' ideas about intelligence.

In a parallel theme that is more pervasive and yet more subtle, public school teachers have been wrestling away from psychologists the mantle of defining what learning is and how it is done. Teachers had grown quite disillusioned with the touted research of famous psychologists about what should work with students in classrooms. After many years of being criticized for not teaching in ways that reflect the researchers' ideas of teaching and learning, public school teachers have joined with philosophers and a different group of psychologists in claiming that students construct their understanding. This constructivist view of the world is popular among teachers and professors of education. Many learning theorists in psychology still maintain rather traditional views of how students learn. Those in society who determine the views of intelligence and learning theory that are institutionally supported are the most influential political groups in all of public education. For many years, the IQ-based definition dominated the scene and was widely accepted by the general populace. However, since 1983, the de facto control over the application of definitions of intelligence (giftedness) and learning theory has ostensibly shifted from academics in universities to professional educators in public schools.

It will be fascinating over the next 20 years to monitor the most recent popular topic of research drawing considerable attention from researchers, professional educators, and lay people alike: brain-based research. While I am personally optimistic that important findings will be yielded from this line of research, we will undoubtedly have to live through periods of time when pedestrian notions of the research will affect classroom practices. For example, brain hemisphericity was the topic of many articles in the popular press some years ago, as were books on teaching to a child's right brain or left brain.

This "movement" was so influential that teachers would describe children as "right-brained" or "left-brained."

The next major event reflects the evolution of pedagogy, changing from a rather inflexible practice of grade skipping to the various options that have been created over the past 40 years or so. Gifted education was not very appealing to parents and teachers when they worried that the only option for little Janie was for her to skip a grade or grades. Today, teachers have myriad options that include grade skipping, teaching techniques that attempt to differentiate the curriculum, and state-funded residential schools. Other options include Saturday and summer programs such as Governor's Schools, and the various talent search programs. While the impetus behind these examples is quite different, I believe that the second set of options (differentiation) will continue to attract supporters among school personnel. The attraction is the result of two things: (a) teachers are the primary decision makers when curricular differentiation is being implemented, and (b) it fits the inclusive model of education toward which many public schools are moving. Two important undercurrents to the support of an inclusion model of instruction are that it has a face validity of egalitarianism and that the term *gifted* is not used. Other historical events have accelerated the acceptance of differentiation. For example, after some early problems with the notion of gifted education, the middle school movement has warmed up to differentiation due to the relentless work of professionals like Carol Tomlinson who have presented at numerous conferences and written books that translate the tenets of differentiation into attractive language for general educators and administrators. Another factor important to this equation is the inclusion movement. Curricular differentiation makes great sense in heterogeneous classrooms.

Another recent event that has had an impact on gifted education has come from the confluence of several situations. The funding of Jacob Javits legislation and the subsequent birth of the National Research Center on the Gifted and

Talented have brought increased attention to the needs of gifted students. Increased research and publications have also been an important by-product of these events. At the same time, the National Association for Gifted Children and the Council for Exceptional Children's Division—The Association for the Gifted have joined together to influence politicians about the nature and needs of gifted students. These two groups have also worked in collaboration with numerous other important professional educational groups to influence the national educational agenda relative to gifted education.

I believe that the changing demographic make-up of people in the United States has had an important impact on the thinking in gifted education over the past 20 years or so. I also believe that the influence will eventually have the greatest impact of any single event or circumstance. As the dominant group in our society that has been serviced directly by gifted education (Caucasian, middle-class males) grows ever smaller in the demographic equation, the more power other groups will have. Although the field of gifted education is still quite inadequate in applying some of the contemporary conceptions of giftedness, the issues surrounding them are being discussed, intellectual restlessness is present, and conflicting ideas are omnipresent. In essence, the stage has been set for many of the nontraditional ideas for defining giftedness, identifying gifted children, and providing services for them to be tested and researched. It will be interesting to see if another type of civil rights movement emerges that is driven by the notion of maximizing the school-related talent of all gifted children. If this type of movement gains momentum, I doubt that the way to resolve the historic disparities among groups of gifted children will be based on psychometric tweaking of instruments. Implicit in these comments is the argument from the critical theory perspective that benefits made available to a society's children reflect the current power structure. Enhancing the opportunities for underrepresented gifted children will require

a type of revolution. Whether the field of gifted education has the ability or will to change practices to the extent that it creates the same degree of potential for maximizing all gifted children's abilities is doubtful. However, many bright, dedicated people from various backgrounds are working hard to bring about those opportunities. Changing the basic structure of our schooling practices is a difficult thing to accomplish. Of course, the proving ground for many of these experiments may very well be in regular classroom settings.

I have chosen to end this chapter by cataloging some of the other trends and issues that I expect to have an effect on the direction and progress of the field of gifted education over the next 50 years. Other mediating trends may include: our confused notions of what giftedness is; the nation's economy; site-based management; individual school boards; national legislation; the evolution of computers and their effect on the practices of schooling; the politicization of schooling; and the goals of schooling. I think the goals we hold for our schools are largely met. I believe that, if we truly expected our schools to maximize the potential of all gifted students by educating learned people who can function well in a democracy, many aspects of our schools would change. Because our society holds confused views about gifted students, gifted students necessarily receive mixed messages every day of their lives. The people who hold these confused views include all walks of life, from architects, to physicians, to teachers, to teacher trainers, and even to the gifted students themselves. I believe that, until a coherent message about giftedness can be crafted that opens doors for the greatest number of gifted children rather than letting only a very small number through, then society will remain discontented with schooling. Some prescribe a panacea of school choice as a remedy for their criticisms of our public schools. The criticisms are representative of one aspect of the problems with which schools struggle in trying to educate gifted students. That is, under this prescription, children are treated as commodities, as capital for

our nation's economy. There is benefit to students becoming employable, but wouldn't it be nice if our goal was to educate people to be the best people they can be?

References

Buescher, T. (1985). A framework for understanding the social and emotional development of gifted and talented students. *Roeper Review, 8,* 10–15.

Coleman, L. J. (1985). *Schooling the gifted.* New York: Addison-Wesley.

Coleman, L. J., & Cross, T. L. (1988). Is being gifted a social handicap? *Journal for the Education of the Gifted,11,* 41–56.

Cross, T. L., Coleman, L. J., & Terhaar-Yonkers, M. (1991). The social cognition of gifted adolescents in schools: Managing the stigma of giftedness. *Journal for the Education of the Gifted, 15,* 44–55.

Cross, T., Cook, R., & Dixon, D. (1996). Psychological autopsies of three academically talented adolescents who committed suicide. *Journal of Secondary Gifted Education*, 403–409.

Davidson, L., & Linnoila, M. (1991). *Risk factors for youth suicide*. Washington, DC: NIMH.

Delisle, J. (1986). Death with honors: Suicide and the gifted adolescent. *Journal of Counseling and Development, 64*, 558–560.

Ebert, B. (1987). Guide to conducting a psychological autopsy. *Professional Psychology: Research and Practice, 18*, 52–56.

Gardner, H. (1983). *Frames of mind*. New York: BasicBooks.

Jones, D. (1977). Suicide by aircraft: A case report. *Aviation, Space, and Environmental Medicine, 48*, 454– 459.

Kaiser, C. F., & Berndt, D. J. (1985). Predictors of loneliness in the gifted adolescent. *Gifted Child Quarterly, 29*, 74–77.

Ludwig, A. L. (1995). *The price of greatness: Resolving the creativity and madness controversy*. New York: Guilford.

May, R. (1969). The emergence of existential psychology. In R. May (Ed.), *Existential psychology* (pp. 1–48). New York: Random House.

Mead, M. (1970). *Culture and commitment*. Garden City, NY: Natural History Press.

Neill, K., Benensohn, H., Farber, A., & Resnick, H. (1974). The psychological autopsy: A technique for investigating a hospital suicide. *Hospital and Community Psychiatry, 25*, 33–36.

Piechowski, M. (1979). Developmental potential. In N. Colangelo & T. Zaffron (Eds.), *New voices in counseling the gifted* (pp. 25–58). Dubuque, IA: Kendall/Hunt.

Terman, L. M. (1925). *Genetic studies of genius: Vol. 1. Mental and physical traits of a thousand gifted children.* Stanford, CA: Stanford University Press.

Tomlinson-Keasy, C., & Keasy, B. (1988). "Signatures" of suicide. In D. Capuzzi & L. Golden (Eds.), *Preventing adolescent suicide* (pp. 213–245). Muncie, IN: Accelerated Development.

Ullman, E. (2000, May). Wouldn't you rather be at home? The Internet and the myth of the powerful self. Lecture excerpted in *Harper's, 300*(1800), 30–33.